LOVE'S GENTLE PROMISE

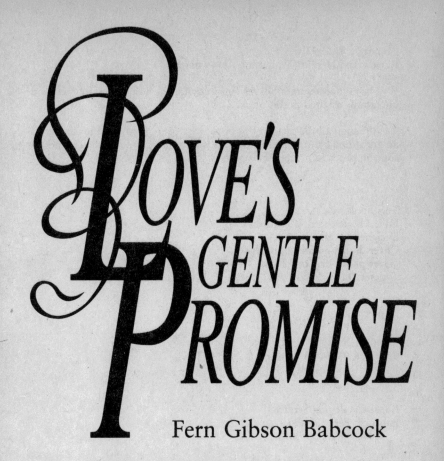

LOVE'S GENTLE PROMISE

Fern Gibson Babcock

REVIEW AND HERALD® PUBLISHING ASSOCIATION
HAGERSTOWN, MD 21740

The author assumes full responsibility for the accuracy of all facts and quotations as cited in this book.

Although all the facts in this book are true and most of the characters are identified by their real names, the author has given assumed names to some in order to protect their privacy.

This book was
Edited by Richard W. Coffen
Designed by Bill Kirstein
Cover design by Steve Trapero
Cover photo by Todd Park
Typeset: 11/12 Sabon

PRINTED IN U.S.A.

98 97 96 95 94 93   10 9 8 7 6 5 4 3 2 1

R&H Cataloging Service
Babcock, Fern Gibson
    Love's gentle promise.

    1. Brown, Marion. I. Title.
            [B]

ISBN 0-8280-0661-X

This book is
lovingly dedicated to
Marion,
whose life reflects the courage of her Master,
to Ed,
whose untiring service
drew many to Jesus Christ,
and to Kenneth,
whose compassionate caring continues
to reveal his Lord.

Contents

CHAPTER

1

Sitting on the edge of the old Chevy's front seat, Marion peered anxiously over the dashboard at the twisting Connecticut road. In all her 9 years, she had never been so nervous. Today of all days, why did her right cheek have to start twitching again? What if the Holmbergs didn't like her? What if they decided not to adopt her?

"I hope you realize how important this interview is, Marion." Mrs. Norris glanced at the girl's rigid back. "You must really be nice to Mrs. Holmberg. If she'll keep you, you won't have to go back to the Litches' again."

Marion didn't answer. She didn't feel like herself at all. Her social worker had arrived at the Litches' with a bag of brand-new clothes, had dressed her from head to foot, and had even put a ribbon in her hair. The white cuffs of her new blue coat hung a little long on her arms, but Mrs. Norris said she looked lovely. Marion couldn't remember anyone ever before saying she looked lovely.

♥ ♥ ♥

Mrs. Litch thought the whole procedure was a bunch of nonsense, of course. "Nobody's going to want that kid no matter how you fancy her up," she told the social worker. "Look at her! Skinny as a rail, nervous as a cat, and moody too. This child isn't easy to handle, you know. I think we've done real well keepin' her for the past six years.

"If those folks do decide to take her, though, I hope you'll remember what a good foster home we've been and bring us another youngster soon. To be perfectly honest, with business as poor as it's been lately, we need the little bit we get from these welfare kids to keep us goin'."

Mrs. Norris nodded. "I know you need the money," she said, "and as for Marion, we'll just have to wait and see what happens, won't we? I do think she looks quite attractive today."

Mrs. Litch snorted. "Peak-ed is more like it," she snapped. "Peak-ed as usual!"

Mrs. Norris picked up Marion's suitcase with one hand and reached for the child with the other. At the foot of the steps she paused and turned, squeezing Marion's hand lightly. "Tell Mrs. Litch goodbye, dear," she prompted.

Marion stared at the ground. "Goodbye," she mumbled.

As Mrs. Litch started down the steps toward the girl, Marion ducked and threw up a protective arm. The woman stopped and laughed. "I'm not goin' to hit you, child. I was fixin' to hug you goodbye. See there, Mrs. Norris? Six years of hard work and not so much as a thank you. Must be in her blood. They say her father was a tough one too."

Marion could feel Mrs. Litch's eyes boring into her. She shuddered. Mrs. Norris' hand tightened on hers. "Come, dear, we must be going. Thank you, Mrs. Litch. Have a nice day." The social worker turned and led Marion to the car.

♥ ♥ ♥

Now they were on their way to Rocky Hill, 10 long miles away, and Mrs. Norris was wondering if Marion knew the importance of this interview.

Of course she knew. If the Holmbergs adopted her, she'd never have to go back to the Litches' again. Finally, she'd be free of Mrs. Litch's spankings, Tommy's pinches, and Susan's demands.

She'd miss old Grandma, of course. Mrs. Litch's mother dipped snuff, sneezed, and coughed a lot, but she'd never tormented Marion like the rest of them, even though she'd had to share a room with her. She'd even taught Marion how to sew on buttons. But Grandma wasn't worth staying at the Litches' for. Nobody was worth that!

Suddenly the car began to slow. "Straighten your bow, dear," Mrs. Norris instructed. "This is the Holmbergs' house. Isn't it lovely?"

Marion squinted as she focused on the neat white house framed by shade trees. The front featured a large enclosed porch, and gable windows hinted at an attic. The nearby houses seemed friendly and reassuring. But when the car glided to a stop, Marion felt panic rising inside. Any minute now she'd be meeting Mrs. Holmberg. What would she be like? Would she be fussy and particular? Would she be kind? Or did she believe in beating kids to get the bad out of them? The child trembled.

"Get out, dear," Mrs. Norris was saying, holding the door open and reaching for Marion's hand.

Good. Although Marion didn't usually like people to touch her, right now she appreciated a friendly hand.

A round motherly woman with dark hair and blue eyes bustled out of the house, across the porch, and opened the door. "Did you bring Marion?" she asked eagerly.

Mrs. Norris nodded at the child. "I certainly did, Mrs. Holmberg. Here she is."

During the next, long minute, Marion kept her eyes fixed on her new shoes. Mrs. Norris watched as the woman's face fell, and her blue eyes filled with consternation. "*That's* Marion?" she asked, puzzled. "But how old is she? She must be 6 at least."

"Nine," Mrs. Norris said. "She's small for her age."

Marion ducked her head, trying to hide her twitching cheek. *Mrs. Holmberg doesn't like me. She must have wanted someone younger. Most people do. Everyone likes babies and toddlers.*

"Uh, this isn't quite what I expected." The lady twisted her apron nervously. "We thought . . . that is . . . her grandmother told us . . . uh—Mrs. Norris, could we talk privately?"

Mrs. Norris set the suitcase inside the porch door and turned, releasing the child's hand. "Marion, honey, could you just walk around the yard a little bit while I talk to Mrs. Holmberg? We won't be long."

"There's a garden out back and a path that goes down to a little creek," Mrs. Holmberg added eagerly. "Go right around the side of the house. You'll see it."

Marion shuffled reluctantly toward the corner as the two women disappeared inside the house. "I'm terribly sorry," Mrs. Holmberg was saying, "but there's been an awful mistake. The girl's great-grandmother, who goes to our church, told me that the child was about 3 years old. We've never had children, Mrs. Norris, and you must understand that we'd planned to kind of start at the beginning. I really thought we'd be stretching it to take a 3-year-old. But 9? It's out of the question! Don't you have any babies who need a good home?"

Mrs. Norris swallowed hard, thinking of Marion's face. The girl already sensed she wasn't wanted. Wouldn't anything go right for this child? "I'm sorry too," commented Mrs. Norris. "When you called and asked that I bring her here, I thought you knew all about her. Her great-grandmother is getting a bit senile, and I suppose she just forgot that children grow. The last time she saw her, I think, was about six years ago. She was 3, then."

Mrs. Holmberg shook her head sorrowfully, but the social worker kept on speaking. "Isn't there any way you could give Marion a chance?" she pleaded. "She needs love more than any child I have right now. She's never really had any, you know. That's why she's so thin and nervous, I'm sure. I've had her in several homes, and this last one has some teenagers who, I'm convinced, have been tormenting the child. I watched them order her around, scolding her no matter what she did. That's when I determined to get her out of there. Your request came just in time."

Mrs. Norris leaned forward and continued earnestly, "I don't plan to put any more children in that home. When Marion was taken to the doctor for a cut to her head, he reported that she had been spanked for falling off the porch and cutting herself! I know she's older than you wanted, but she's very small for a 9-year-old. Couldn't you at least give her a try? She was so excited about coming here that I'm afraid a rejection will just crush her."

Mrs. Holmberg turned and stared out the window. "I'm truly sorry about the child," she began in a distressed voice, "but adoption is too big a step to take lightly. Andy and I were prepared to take in a 3-year-old—a cute, cuddly child who would bring love and laughter into our home. This one is way too old and obviously has some emotional problems besides. I just don't see how we . . ."

"AAAAAAAGGGGGGHHHH! Help! A snake! A snake! *Hel-l-l-p*!" Earsplitting screams erupted from the back garden.

Mrs. Holmberg leaped to her feet and ran out the back door, the social worker right behind. Down the steps and along the path they flew toward the hysterical child.

"What *is* it?" Mrs. Norris shouted. "Be still, Marion!"

"A snake!" screamed the girl. "It's gonna get me! Don't let him get me! *Help*!"

Suddenly they saw a black form slithering on the ground in front of the petrified child.

Realizing that Marion couldn't move, Mrs. Norris

grabbed her from behind and dragged her back. Mrs. Holmberg fled across the street. "Mr. Austin! Mr. Austin!" she shouted. "Come quick! A snake!"

A heavyset man with a hoe in his hand left his flower bed and ran to the Holmbergs' backyard. In a minute the snake's spastic body was stretched out on the path, as Mr. Austin gave it a few final blows with his hoe. "That's a big one," he commented. "Must be three feet at least."

But the ladies weren't listening. Both women were frantically trying to quiet the hysterical girl, whose face was hidden in Mrs. Norris' skirt. "There, there, it's dead. It's all taken care of," Mrs. Norris soothed.

"I'm *so* sorry," Mrs. Holmberg said as she dried the girl's tears with the edge of her apron. "We've never had a snake before, or I wouldn't have sent you out here. What a terrible fright! Do stop crying, dear."

As Marion's sobs subsided, Mrs. Holmberg's heart softened. "How would you like to spend the night with me?" she asked, stooping to Marion's level. "Just tonight, you understand. Since you've brought your suitcase, you might as well stay over. Mrs. Norris can pick you up again tomorrow. We'll have some of my special Swedish pancakes with strawberry jam for supper. Would you like that?"

Although Marion had never had Swedish pancakes before, her imagination conjured them up immediately—stacks of thin, melt-in-your-mouth delicacies dripping with sweet red jam. Staring groundward, she nodded.

Mrs. Norris sighed with relief and straightened up. "That's settled then," she said, smiling gratefully. "I'll be back tomorrow. And thank you, Mrs. Holmberg. Thank you very much."

After the old Chevy had pulled away from the curb, Mrs. Holmberg showed Marion a neat little bedroom just off the kitchen. "This was our bedroom," she explained, "but we moved up to the attic last night so you'd have a room of your own. Uh—not *you*, actually, but the child we plan to adopt. You can sleep there tonight, though. Why don't you take your coat off and help me make pancakes?"

Shyly the girl removed her coat and laid it on the pink bedspread. Then she drifted slowly over to stand in the doorway and watched the woman bustle about in the kitchen. Before long she found herself sifting flour, beating eggs, and not actually talking, but listening a lot as the Swedish woman rambled on about all the good food in her homeland.

Just as Marion had begun to relax, the back door burst open. A man with jet black hair and kind eyes stood in the doorway, his six-foot frame filling it completely. "Well, well, what have we here?" he asked jovially.

"This is Mr. Holmberg, Marion," the woman said. "Marion's spending the night with us, Andy. Just the night."

Andy gave his wife a questioning glance but stooped to pat Marion's head. "That's nice," he said. "Looks like we're having your special pancakes, Cora. I'll get washed up and be right out."

At the table, the Holmbergs bowed their heads while Marion watched, frowning. "Bow your head, dear," Cora instructed her. "We thank God for our food before we eat it."

Oh. She'd heard of that once in Sunday school, but she'd never seen it done. Obediently she bowed her head.

After a simple blessing, Cora piled two golden pancakes on Marion's plate and reached for the jam.

"Do you give jam to welfare kids?" Marion asked hopefully. "Litches don't. They say welfare doesn't pay enough for jam. Only Susan and Tommy get jam."

Mrs. Holmberg bristled. "Well, of all things! Of *course* you get jam, dear. You get anything we get." Her eyes indignantly sought Andy's.

He shook his head almost imperceptibly, warning her to

be still. "What grade are you in, Marion?" he asked gently as he poured her a glass of milk. "I'll bet you're a good student, aren't you? Did you meet our little dog Tudy? She's watchin' every bite you take. She'd like some of your pancake, but we don't feed her at the table."

By bedtime Mr. Holmberg had gotten quite a bit of information from his young guest. Yes, she liked dogs, but the people she'd lived with didn't have any. She'd lived with the Litches six years. She was in the third grade now. The scar on her cheek came from a cut she'd gotten when the railing on the second floor porch gave way and she had plummeted to the rocks below. The doctor had put in six stitches, but that didn't hurt as much as the spanking Mrs. Litch had given her for leaning on the railing. She had shared a room with Grandma. Susan made her run errands a lot. Tommy pinched her. Mrs. Litch wouldn't let her eat liverwurst like the other kids. It was like jam. Not for welfare kids.

In spite of her shyness, Andy had a gentle way of getting all sorts of information out of the child.

When supper was over, Mrs. Holmberg helped Marion get ready for bed. Her outer clothes had been new, but her old nightgown had a few holes in it. Embarrassed, Marion jumped quickly into bed and pulled up the covers.

"Don't you want to say your prayers, dear?" Mrs. Holmberg asked anxiously.

Marion shook her head. The woman sighed. "Oh well, I don't suppose you know how, do you? Why don't you just shut your eyes, and I'll say a prayer for you." And she did. When she was finished, she tucked the bedding a little tighter around Marion's neck, giving her just a hint of a goodnight pat as she did so. "Tudy sleeps in the kitchen, dear, so if you hear her scratching around, don't be alarmed. I'll leave the door ajar a bit so you'll have just a little light, OK?"

When Mrs. Holmberg had gone, Marion felt all trembly again. Never before had she slept in a room alone, much less one so neat and tidy. And never had anyone prayed for her. The snake, the dog, the pancakes, the jam—she fell asleep thinking about the jam.

♥ ♥ ♥

That night before she slipped into bed, Cora Holmberg tiptoed in to check on her guest. The child looked very small and defenseless in the big bed. *If only she were 3, there'd be no question about her staying,* Cora told herself.

Upstairs she and Andy discussed the situation, concluding that Cora was right. Marion must go back tomorrow. They'd wait for a toddler.

Hardly had the two adults dropped off to sleep when blood-curdling screams and Tudy's barking jolted them awake again. Andy leaped from bed and bounded downstairs. Cora was close behind. Sobbing and gasping, Marion was sitting upright in bed.

"The snake's got me," she screamed. "Don't let him get me. The snake! The snake!"

Cora swept past Andy and gathered the girl in her arms. "There, there," she soothed, "wake up, child. It's just a bad dream. The snake's dead. Mr. Austin killed it. Remember? He buried it down by the creek. It can't get you now. Besides, we asked the Lord to protect you tonight, and the angels are right here with you. But you'd better stop crying now. You're upsetting poor Tudy terribly. Here, pet her and let her know you're OK."

The woman guided Marion's hand to the dog's head. The warm fur distracted the child, and her sobbing gradually subsided. The trembling, however, continued. She couldn't stop it.

"Would you feel better if I stayed down here with you tonight?" Cora asked.

Head down, the girl nodded. Cora's eyes met Andy's, and he turned and went back upstairs alone. Tucking Marion into bed again, Cora climbed into the twin bed beside it and settled down for the night.

Long after Marion's regular breathing told Cora she was asleep, the woman lay awake wondering about this child. She certainly wasn't 3. She didn't fit the picture Cora had had in her mind at all, the picture of a happy, cuddly toddler. But holding her tonight as she sobbed and trembled, Cora had felt the first stirrings of mother love. This child needed her. Anyone this insecure needed all the love she could get. Cora knew Andy would agree. She'd seen his face as he watched the child's terror.

During that wakeful night Cora decided. Never mind the age. They would keep Marion.

2

When Marion joined Mr. and Mrs. Holmberg, only six weeks of the school year remained. Rather than transporting her back to the Elmwood school near the Litches, Cora and Andy decided to put her in a nearby public school for the last few weeks.

"Would you like that, dear?" Cora inquired. "I know you'll miss your old friends at Elmwood, but you'll soon make new ones here I'm sure."

Marion nodded solemnly. "Oh, yes. I don't have any friends at Elmwood anyway. The kids there tease me and say I don't have a father. I told them I did so, and he'd come and see me. But he never did, and they just laughed. I'd rather go to school here."

So Cora enrolled her daughter in third grade at Rocky Hill Elementary and wondered how it would work out. The child seemed so eager to be going to a new school but frightened as well.

The first school day, she arrived home ready to quit. "I can't do math in this school," she told Andy that night. "I don't know what on earth they're talking about. The teacher said they were doing long division, whatever that is, and that I should know my times tables. What are times tables?"

Andy looked astonished. "Times tables? They're like two times three is six. You know. What's two times two?"

With a blank look, Marion shook her head. "I don't know," she confessed.

"Then I guess you'll have to learn," he concluded. "We need to get you caught up so you'll be right with the other kids next year. We might as well get started."

Andy disappeared upstairs and returned with some old arithmetic books. The two of them sat down at the kitchen table. Although Andy had finished only eight grades of school, he had a good understanding of math. Now he explained multiplication to Marion, who listened intently, her thin forehead furrowed in concentration. Before the evening was over she knew the ones and twos in the times tables.

After having had no father at all, the child delighted in the attention she received from this big, kind man, who so obviously cared about her. Because they were typically reserved New Englanders, the Holmbergs seldom hugged each other or Marion, but coming from the same background, Marion neither gave nor expected much physical affection. For her it was enough that her new father came home from work every day during those first few months with some small gift for her—a balloon, a tiny notebook, a shiny dime, a chocolate bar.

Marion began sitting on the front steps, where she watched eagerly for his return each night. She'd struggle to keep her impatience well hidden until Andy shyly produced from his big pocket the day's surprise.

"Here, kiddo, have some peanuts." Andy would toss the nickel bag into the air, and laughing with delight, Marion would catch it. Other times she'd run to meet him, slipping her small hand into his as they walked the last block home. When she held Andy's hand, Marion felt a strange security and peace. Occasionally she even slowed her pace so that she could hold on longer. Sometimes when he gave her a treat, she would voice her thanks, but more often the big man only received a grateful look. He understood, however. It was the New England way.

After supper each night, Andy drilled Marion on her times tables for a full hour. Before long she began to catch up with her classmates at school, and by the end of the year she was ready to go on to fourth grade. The math drill didn't stop with the end of school, however, but continued all summer long. By September Marion could easily hold her own in the class.

Stiffly at first and then with increasing ease, Marion found herself calling Andy "Dad" and Cora "Mother." Then, during the summer, she began to realize what a big family she had gotten into. Cora's brother Grover lived right across the street. Doris and Irene, two of Cora's sisters, resided in a house on one side of the Holmbergs, while a third sister, Blanche, lived on the other side and shared her home with their mother. Marion learned to love Grandma Johnson, who, in turn, enjoyed the child's company. Together they passed many pleasant summer hours.

Right from the start, Cora took her daughter to Sabbath school and church every Saturday. Marion soon learned that although Dad did not believe in the Adventist religion, which Cora had embraced, he still respected it and encouraged his wife and daughter to attend. He himself went off to work as usual each Saturday morning and repaired teletypewriters at the telephone company.

Andy had no objections, either, when Cora decided to enroll Marion at the little Adventist school in Hartford. True, it was 10 miles away, but she could ride with Aunt Blanche when she went to work in the morning and could come home on the city bus.

"I won't have to go alone the first day, will I?" she asked Cora anxiously. "When I was at the Litches' they sent me off to first grade all alone. I didn't even know how to get into the building. I sat down and cried, and my nose bled, and I went home. But Mrs. Litch spanked me. Can you come with me the first day?"

Cora's face registered her indignation, but she only said, "Of course! I'll go with you and show you how to get home on the trolley and bus. You'll like the Adventist school, Marion. It's very small—only one teacher for all the grades. I think they have 14 students this year. You'll soon know all of them."

Reassured that this time she didn't have to handle everything alone, Marion relaxed and found the new school very enjoyable indeed, and there she found her first real friend—Stephanie. Although her classmate lived in a different town, the two girls managed to get together for weekends and occasional outings. Marion loved playing the piano at Stephanie's house or going out back to visit the goats. Drinking goat milk, however, was something else, and although she tried it, Marion never really enjoyed its taste.

Cora's relatives delighted in showering affection on the love-starved child. Having so many aunts and uncles was wonderful—especially that first Christmas. Beneath the Holmbergs' tree a mountain of gifts accumulated for Marion—puzzles, clothes, games, books, and a complete family of dolls. The child's delight warmed the hearts of the whole family. "Are these *all* for *me*, Mother?" she asked wonderingly.

"Certainly. Haven't you had Christmas presents before?"

Marion thought, then replied, "Yes, I did once. The last year I was at Litches' I got a little pocketbook and a fur muff. But that was the first Christmas I got things. I think Mr. Litch got them for me. Susan and Tommy had lots of presents, but I usually got just a candy cane. I guess the welfare money wasn't enough to buy presents for me."

Cora's lips set in a firm line. "Well, you aren't a welfare child anymore. You're our daughter. And *everybody* in the family gets presents at Christmastime."

Gradually Marion learned about giving and receiving and began to experience the fun of sneaking around to surprise someone with a special gift.

That spring brought a hurricane—right in the middle of a school day. Someone called the school and advised the teacher to send her students home at once. Marion scurried to the trolley and began her 10-mile trip home, changing to the bus en route. Passengers peered anxiously out the darkening windows at the increasing wind. At the top of a hill near her home, Marion got off and began running for home.

Suddenly a fierce gust blew her off her feet and tore the hat from her head. Crying in fright, she struggled against the wind, fighting her way home. On the enclosed porch, Cora waited. Relief filled her face when her daughter came into sight. She ran down the walk with a big poncho, pulling Marion inside with her. Back on the porch, Cora enfolded the child in her arms and calmed her down. Marion relaxed, grateful for the unaccustomed hug as much as for security from the storm.

Andy, however, was not safely inside. All that day and for three more after it, the repairman worked to restore telephone service to Hartford. Although rain torrents had flooded the city, Andy found a rowboat and rowed from one place to another, repairing downed lines and evacuating people from flooded homes.

With her usual concern for others, Cora took in stranded commuters who couldn't make it home. All the excitement and activity, added to several days out of school, made the hurricane episode one that Marion would never forget.

Before long the girl made friends with Grover's boys, Raymond and Roger, who lived across the street. Although the boys were kept close to home and not really encouraged to socialize with Marion, they were allowed to play with her sometimes. The questions they asked their new cousin prompted her to quiz Cora. "Mother, Roger asked where my father is. Do you know?"

"No, child, I can't say that I do. His name is Charles Brainard, though, and he was married to your mother, Dorothy. You have a brother, Chuck, who's a little older than you. Your father's parents are raising him."

The girl's voice quivered with excitement. "I've got a brother? Why aren't we together?"

Cora sighed. She'd rather not go into all of this, but the child had a right to know something, she supposed. "Your parents were living together when Chuck was born," she explained. "Then before you arrived, your father ran off. Your mother, Dorothy, got sick, so she let Social Services care for you. Your father's mother thought taking care of Chuck was enough. Your mother's in a tuberculosis hospital now, I believe, but I don't know where your father is. He was not a good father or a good husband, and I just pray that you inherited none of his traits. Shiftless and irresponsible, that's what he was."

Marion winced. The truth hurt.

"I found you through Grandma Holmes. She goes to our church, you know. She's really your great-grandmother. She was worried about your mother and her children, and when I was talking about adopting a child, she remembered you. I think it was in the Lord's plan that you come here. We needed you and you needed us."

Since Marion had joined the Holmberg family, she saw Great-grandmother Holmes nearly every week when Cora picked her up to attend church. The child's size shocked the old lady at first, but she soon adjusted. Before long the girl was a frequent visitor in the big old house where Great-grandmother lived with her daughter Essie. Since there were several skeletons in the family closet, Essie felt it best that no one discuss Marion's background.

Great-grandmother Holmes, however, felt otherwise.

One day when Marion was visiting, Essie stepped out to the store. "Now that she's gone," the old lady whispered, "come back to my room, and I'll show you some family pictures."

In the bedroom, Marion stared, fascinated. Here were pictures of her Grandpa Holmes and his daughter, Marion's mother. And here was her father, Charles—young, handsome, and carefree. He looked so nice it was hard to believe he'd abandoned her mother and two children. As she stared, she felt resentment rising. Who did he think he was, dumping them all like that?

Without warning, Aunt Essie burst into the bedroom, snatched the album, and faced her mother with blazing eyes. "I *told* you not to fill this child's head with nonsense, Mother. What's done is done. There's no need to rehash it. Now you come into the living room, both of you. There's a new *National Geographic* on the table, if you want pictures to look at."

For years afterward, Marion wondered what else she might have learned if Essie hadn't interrupted.

While the girl appreciated her new home more than her parents could know, she didn't always show it. During the next two years she began to lose her shyness and started asserting a new independence that wasn't at all pleasing to Cora. Some days she seemed rebellious from the time she awoke. Knowing the girl's heritage, Cora constantly worried that Charles Brainard's wild and shiftless ways might show up in his daughter. She resolved to firmly squash any such tendencies.

One afternoon after Marion had supposedly done the dishes, her mother discovered an unwashed pan in the cupboard. "Marion," she called, "come right here!"

Marion strolled into the kitchen.

"Why is this dirty pan in the cupboard?"

The child cocked her head to one side. "Because I put it there," she answered saucily.

Cora gasped. "Marion, I won't put up with that! I told you to wash the dishes. This is a dirty, sneaky trick, the sort of thing your father might have done. It's the Brainard coming out in you, and I won't have it, do you understand?"

Marion's face reddened in anger. "I *am* a Brainard, whether you like it or not. And I *hate* washing your dirty pots and pans. Sometimes I think you just took me so I could do all your dirty work!"

As the blood drained from Cora's face, Andy stepped into the kitchen. He had overheard the whole episode. "Marion!" he thundered. "You have no right to speak to your mother like that. You ought to be spanked. We've been good to you and loved you like our own child, but if we'd had one, we would have spanked her by now, I'm sure. Come with me, young lady, and take your punishment. Then you'll come back and scrub that pan until you can see your face in it!"

Marion set her jaw firmly. "I will *not*," she shouted. "I'm 11 years old, and I won't be spanked!"

Andy dived for the girl, but she dodged out of reach. He took off right after her, chasing her around and around the kitchen table.

"Andy, *stop it*!" Cora shouted. "Get hold of yourself. We can't settle anything this way."

But Andy, usually so quiet and amiable, was aroused now and wouldn't stop. "I'll settle something all right. I'll settle this girl down if I ever get hold of her. Come here, Marion!" He stopped for breath and glared at her.

Flushed with her success, Marion grinned mockingly. "I'm faster than you!" she panted.

Cora sucked in her breath in one gasp, shot forward, and grabbed the child from behind. With one hand she held her and with the other smacked her face left and right in fury. Marion's screams filled the kitchen, the same frantic screams that had erupted the night of the snake nightmare.

Andy's shoulders sagged. "Stop it!" he ordered. "Cora, stop it!"

Cora released her grip, and Marion fled to her room. She knew she deserved punishment, but Mother had no right to say such things about the Brainard family. Maybe it was true, though. Maybe there *was* too much of Charles Brainard in her. How could a girl know who she was with such a mixed-up background? And where would she go if the Holmbergs turned her out?

Later that night when Cora came to tuck her daughter into bed, Marion made peace. "I'm sorry, Mother. I don't know what got into me. I won't leave the dirty pans anymore, but could you please not say things about the Brainards? Maybe they're true, but I don't like to hear them. OK?"

Cora's eyes filled with tears. "I'm sorry, too, Marion. I completely lost my temper. I know the Lord is ashamed of me, and I've asked His forgiveness. Now I need yours. Can you forgive me? What you did was wrong, but what I did was worse."

Marion reached up to give her mother a rare hug, and as Cora returned it warmly peace settled over the Holmberg home again.

The best part of living at Holmbergs, Marion thought, was the summer. Aunt Blanche and Andy both owned cottages in Maine. During the summer the brothers and sisters of the large Swedish family took turns staying at the seacoast town of Glenmere. While others went back to work after their vacations, Marion stayed with whatever group of relatives was left. She swam daily, walked by the sea, or cycled back and forth between the two cottages. During her twelfth year she made friends with Susan, a girl her own age. Now she had Stephanie at home and Susan in Maine. The closeness of special friends made Marion feel secure.

Perhaps her closest friend, however, was, strangely enough, her Aunt Doris. When the snow fell, Aunt Doris came bustling over and lured her niece into sledding with her down a steep hill. When Andy bought his daughter a bicycle, Doris bought one too so they could go riding together. When Aunt Doris and Susan were both in Maine, Marion's happiness was complete.

Once a week they went into town to "shop." Marion usually had a nickel or dime to spend, and if Andy was there, he was sure to tell her not to "spend it all in one place." Marion would walk the dime store aisles, eagerly calling Susan or Aunt Doris to see one treasure after the other, putting off her actual purchase to prolong the pleasure. At such times Marion forgot she was adopted and really felt she was part of the family.

At other times, however, when Marion heard from her real mother, she didn't know where she belonged. After nearly four years in a tuberculosis sanatorium, where the doctors sometimes despaired of her life, Dorothy had finally been cured. Immediately she went back to school, learned office skills, and landed a good job with an insurance company in Hartford.

Before long she reclaimed her son, Chuck, from his Brainard grandparents and set up housekeeping again. But it was too late to get Marion back. Legal adoption papers had been signed and filed long before. Anyway, whenever Dorothy visited the Holmberg home, she felt certain that Marion was better off there.

While Dorothy kept in touch with the Brainards because they had custody of Chuck, she seldom heard any news of their son Charles, whom she had divorced. So she was certainly startled when he turned up at her Hartford apartment one night. He had, he said, come to see Chuck and Marion.

Dorothy stared at him. See *Marion*? He'd never before asked to see his daughter. From past experience, Dorothy knew that this man left pain wherever he went, and she preferred that her daughter be spared any more.

"Chuck's playing basketball tonight, and Marion lives in Rocky Hill. She's been legally adopted by a family there. How come you care about the kids all of a sudden? You haven't seen Marion in all her 12 years. Why now?"

Charles shrugged. "I don't know. Just thought I'd like to see her. I bought her a sweater and a doll. Show me where she is, and let's see what she thinks of her old man."

Dorothy's face tightened. "Haven't you done enough damage to her already?" she snapped. "Leave her alone. She's happy where she is, and I don't bother her. Now you come along after 12 years and say 'Here's a doll and a sweater, kid. How about a hug for your dear father?' Forget it. I don't want you to see her."

During the next half hour Charles proved that he hadn't been called "The Charmer" for nothing. Before long he and Dorothy were in his car headed for Rocky Hill.

When they knocked at Holmbergs' door, Cora was anything but pleased. For years she had detested this man and what he had done to Marion, and now, smiling and charming, he was trying to push himself back into her life.

"I don't know if Marion wants to see you or not," she said. "She's reading right now. If you'll just wait here on the porch, I'll ask her."

Cora closed the front door and walked into Marion's room. Her voice was tight and unnatural. "Marion, your father is here and wants to see you. Do you want to see him?"

Marion's heart pounded, and she felt suddenly ill. Her *father*? Charles? The one who had rejected her and never seen her in her life? Because of him she'd been teased, passed around to foster homes, and filled with lonely, abandoned feelings. If she met him, she just might tell him what she thought of him. "What should I do, Mother?" she asked, nervously flipping pages.

"Whatever you like," was the reply.

The strange, wary look on Cora's face helped Marion decide. Happier with the Holmbergs than at any other time in her life, she feared to jeopardize her relationship with Cora. Obviously her adopted mother didn't like that man. The girl quickly decided. "I don't want to see him. Tell him I said that."

Relief flashed across her mother's face. She turned and went back to the front door. "Marion refuses to see you," she told Charles, "and I can't say that I blame her."

The man's smile disappeared. Charles held out the doll

and sweater awkwardly. "Uh . . . well, could you at least give her these for me?"

Cora drew herself up sternly. "No, I'd rather not," she said. "The sweater's too small, and she doesn't play with dolls much. I'd rather not upset her, if you don't mind. Good day!" And she shut the door.

Marion sat on her bed and listened to the sound of a car receding in the distance. Part of her longed to see her father. Another part hated him. She had no way of knowing that someday she would regret her one lost opportunity to meet her father.

C H A P T E R

4

Living at the Holmbergs' involved a total change of lifestyle for Marion. At the Litches' she had longed for liverwurst, but that was reserved for family members. Now that she was getting plenty of Cora's good food, meat lost its importance. "I think I want to be a vegetarian," she told Cora one day.

"Good for you," her mother responded. "It's a much healthier diet. Do you think you can stick to it?"

"Sure. Thinking of eating dead animals turns my stomach now. I don't think even a hamburger would taste good!" And Marion was right. Being a vegetarian was no problem, and it was a preference she would maintain for the rest of her life.

Although Andy declined to join them, Cora and Marion had morning worship each day. The budding teenager learned to love this close, quiet time together, and these worships, along with Bible classes at school, led her to think seriously about giving her heart to the Lord. While she was in eighth grade she joined a Friday night baptismal class so she, along with several of her classmates, could prepare to join the Adventist Church.

This delighted Cora since she had no idea that Marion's interest in the Friday night meetings was not entirely spiritual. A handsome high school senior led the song service, and the teenagers often teased him about losing the musical beat while watching Marion. Even though she was just an eighth grader, the song leader found the petite blonde very attractive, and her interest in him was obvious. When Cora found out, she heartily disapproved, of course, and the romance died.

Fortunately, Marion's interest in joining the church flourished anyway, and she announced her decision to be baptized. Cora was very pleased, and Andy thought it was a fine idea. The day of that event, as she reached for Marion's hand to help her out of the water, Cora felt a new closeness to her adopted daughter. Now she was not only part of the Holmberg family, but part of the Adventist family as well.

Since the little Hartford school taught only eight grades, most graduates attended South Lancaster Academy in Massachusetts for high school. The year Marion finished eighth grade, however, several parents decided not to send their eighth-graders away. Instead, they arranged for the local church school teacher to supervise ninth-grade work by correspondence. The Holmbergs liked that idea too, and Marion didn't mind staying home another year since her best friend, Stephanie, was also remaining in Hartford. Together the girls studied, giggled, talked about boys, and planned the fun they'd have later in boarding school.

After another lazy summer at the beach, Marion began packing to go to South Lancaster Academy. Cora could hardly stand the thought of sending her away, but neither could she bear to send her to public school. During the girl's impulsive teen years, Cora definitely wanted her under the influence of Christian teachers.

The exciting prospect of being on her own threw the 16-year-old into a whirl of shopping and sewing. "Can't we put a different collar on this, Mother?" she begged. "And how about shortening my red skirt a bit? Long skirts are so out of style now."

Cora nodded approval. "I think I have a pretty lace collar

Aunt Irene made that would look nice on that dress, but we'd better be careful how short we make the skirt. They have rather strict rules at the academy."

Departure time came all too soon. Loading their teenager and all her belongings into their old Packard, Cora and Andy drove to South Lancaster and placed Marion in the care of the dormitory dean. Before leaving, Marion received a rare hug from her mother. There was no question about her love for her daughter, but Cora simply wasn't a demonstrative person, and hugs were reserved for special occasions. This was one of those times.

Academy life proved vastly different from church school, but Stephanie's familiar presence helped. Everything seemed to be done by the bell. Rise by a bell. Go to worship by a bell. Classes piled on top of one another, bell after bell. Dinner bell. Supper bell. Bedtime bell.

Marion didn't mind so much, but the routine drove Stephanie wild. Sneaking past the dorm monitor during study hall one October evening, Stephanie tiptoed into her friend's room. "If I hear one more bell, I'll go crazy!" she exploded. "I'm sick and tired of being told what to do. We've been here for two months now, and I feel like I've been in jail. The food is horrid. I haven't had a hamburger for *eight* weeks! And today the dean jumped on me about a little lipstick. I'd like to get out of here, wouldn't you?"

Marion's eyed widened in surprise. "No, I like it here. I'm a vegetarian already, so I don't miss hamburgers. And I don't mind the bells. I think it's kind of fun being in the dorm too, even if we didn't get to room together this year. Being in the same dorm with all these college girls kind of makes me feel grown up."

Stephanie frowned. "*Feel* grown up? We *are* grown up, moron. We're 16. Lots of girls are married at 16! We really don't have to stay here, you know."

As Stephanie talked, Marion began to feel that perhaps

the restrictions weren't reasonable after all. The rebellious streak that Cora so often worried about began to assert itself. Before midnight that evening, Marion had agreed to run away with Stephanie the next day.

Early in the morning after their roommates had gone to class, Marion and Stephanie packed their smallest suitcases with absolute necessities, kept a sharp eye out for the dean, and sneaked out the back of the dorm.

"Where are we going?" Marion asked.

"South," Stephanie answered confidently. "Just trust me. We'll go down where it's warmer, get some jobs, and forget this place. Come on!"

Not far from South Lancaster the girls caught a ride with a passing farmer. They invented, for his benefit, a story about having to hurry home to be with a sick mother during surgery. An hour later they stood by the roadside, hitchhiking again.

During the following week the girls continued south. New York, New Jersey, Delaware, Maryland, Virginia, North Carolina. With only $20 between them, motels were out of the question. Most nights were spent riding farther south. One night they slept in the woods, another behind the bushes against an empty house.

As they traveled, Stephanie enjoyed her hamburgers while Marion ate grilled cheese sandwiches until she was sick of them. Even though she was running away, she still couldn't bring herself to eat meat. Most of the time, however, the girls subsisted on crackers and soda.

After the first few days, Marion grew weary of the trip. She hadn't realized how panicky the lack of security would make her feel. She also longed for a hot bath and clean clothes.

"What do you think our folks will do when they catch us?" Marion wondered aloud.

Stephanie laughed. "They'll never catch us. If we're

picked up, we just won't tell our names. No one will be able to trace us, either. We'll just sit tight and get jobs like we planned." Then she turned a fierce face toward Marion. "You aren't going to chicken out, are you? I won't have it. If you tell anybody our real names, I'll kill you. I swear!"

Marion quailed inwardly. Ever since fourth grade Stephanie had been her leader. Whatever her friend suggested, Marion did. She didn't doubt that Stephanie was capable of murder, if it came to that, and clearly the girl meant business!

That afternoon the runaways arrived in Greensboro, North Carolina. In a gas station bathroom they washed up and applied fresh lipstick before going in search of a grocery store. Coming out, they spotted two young men with crew cuts and in uniform lounging against a mailbox at the end of the block.

"Look at that," Stephanie marveled. "If we work it right, there's our supper. Come on, girl, look pretty!"

With Stephanie in the lead, the girls approached the soldiers and began a conversation, giving the boys the now well-worn "mother needs surgery" story. The guys looked amused. After half an hour of banter, they invited the girls out for an evening of fun.

"But first," one said, "we have to call base and check in. We'll be right back."

For 10 minutes the girls waited confidently on the corner. All at once two plainclothes men approached them. "Would you girls step into the hotel lobby?" they asked, flashing badges. "We're military police, and since it looks like you're trying to pick up some of our soldiers, we'd like to ask you a few questions."

Marion's heart pounded. *The police must think we're common prostitutes!*

Stephanie shot Marion a quick glance. "Don't you dare give them our names," she hissed. "I meant what I said."

In the hotel lobby, the officers received no information

from the girls. Frustrated, they walked them down the street and turned them over to the local police. Since they still refused to give their names, the girls were locked in separate cells. Every hour or two an officer tried to question them. By morning, Marion no longer cared about Stephanie's threats. If she'd thought the academy was jail, what on earth was this? With a rush of tears, Marion finally gave the officer their names and addresses.

Back in Rocky Hill, Cora and Andy were frantic. They had been trying to locate Marion ever since the school had reported her disappearance. Andy, a former member of the volunteer police force, had friends following every possible lead. Alerts had gone out to several states, but no one had thought the girls would be so far south. When the Greensboro police called, Cora wept with relief. Marion was alive and safe! But who knew what had happened to her on the trip? Her father's wild streak was certainly coming out in her.

By the time Andy reached North Carolina, the girls had been gone a week and had spent two days in jail. Securing their release, he looked at his daughter sorrowfully. "Marion, what on earth made you do it?"

Sobbing, she threw her arms around her dad's neck. "I don't know," she wept. "Stephanie wanted to run away, so I went with her. I didn't really hate academy. I guess I just wanted an adventure. Please take me home, Daddy!"

On the train back, Andy watched the girls carefully, for Marion had told him, with real fear in her eyes, of Stephanie's threat to kill her. But Stephanie had no chance to do anything with Andy's stern eyes upon her every time she looked up.

When they reached Hartford, Andy handed Stephanie over to her parents. Outside the train station, Cora waited for them by the car. When they appeared, all the week's frustration intensified. Cora's first glimpse of her runaway daughter revealed a very disheveled, dirty teenager still defiantly wearing bright red lipstick.

Something in Cora snapped. Striding forward to meet Marion, she drew back her hand and struck her on the face. "Get that lipstick off!" she shouted. "Don't you have any shame at all? You look like Jezebel! I might have known you'd pull a trick like this. Once a Brainard, always a Brainard. You're no Holmberg. You're a tramp!"

Although she'd put on a good front, Marion had inwardly quailed at the thought of facing her mother. Now, however, rage replaced the fear. "Yes, I *am* a Brainard," she retorted, making no move to wipe off the offending makeup, "and you don't have to keep me any longer. I'll go and live with my own mother. She's right here in Hartford. I can find her. You won't have to put up with me, and I won't have to put up with you and your dumb Adventist religion. I never wanted to be an Adventist anyway. You made me."

Cora paled, but her anger was not yet spent. Coldly she stared at Marion. "I wish you *could* go to your own mother," she snapped. "I called her and asked if she wanted you back, but she said no. You're so bad even your own mother doesn't want you. What am I supposed to do with you? The Holmbergs have never had such goings on in their family. Never! I'm embarrassed to death!"

After the tirade, Andy tried vainly to say a few words, but Cora whirled and stalked to the car, where she sat rigid and unyielding.

Andy walked over to the Packard, leaned in the window, and whispered fiercely, "Leave her alone, Cora. She's been through a lot. She's acting brave, but she's really scared to death. If you keep at her now, we may lose her forever. Lay off!"

Cora did not look at him. "She's hopeless and no good," she retorted. "I don't want even to talk to her. Just take her to the doctor and have her examined. Goodness knows what she's been doing for a week!"

Andy sighed, shook his head in disbelief, then turned back to his daughter and put his arm around her. "Mother's just upset because she was so worried," he told her quietly. "Keep still till she cools off."

The silence at supper was deafening. Andy tried to make conversation, but Cora and Marion hardly spoke and never looked at one another. It was the next day before things began to calm down.

Going back to South Lancaster Academy was out of the question. The school would not take her. Cora applied to Union Springs Academy in New York, and they agreed to accept Marion. But God had other plans.

In her distress, Cora had talked with the Adventist minister, asking him to pray for Marion's safe return. Now that she was back, Pastor Carroll Pike stopped by for a visit. Angry and rebellious toward both her mother and the church, Marion was not pleased by his interest.

He's like everybody else, she thought. *He just wants to know what Stephanie and I did that week. Even the minister wants all the juicy details!*

But to her surprise, Pastor Pike hardly mentioned the episode except to tell her he was glad she was safely back. "What I really came for," he continued, "is to see if you could help us out at the church this quarter. Our Sabbath school secretary transferred to Boston last week, and we're in a bind. I thought that since you were back home now, maybe you could take over the job."

Marion's mind reeled. After all she'd done, he wanted her to be the Sabbath school secretary? The academy knew how terrible she was and refused to have her back. But Elder Pike wanted her back in the church—and even up front, holding an important office. Maybe he didn't understand the situation.

"I don't think you want me for that job," she said. "Don't you know how bad I am? Mother says I'm a regular Jezebel!"

Elder Pike smiled. "No, Marion, I don't think you're really a bad girl at all. You're mischievous, adventurous, and stubborn sometimes, but bad? I think not. You gave your heart to the Lord some time ago, and I think you really love Him and long to do what's right. You're going through some rather hard times right now. The teen years can be miserable ones. I remember, believe it or not. The Lord loves you very much, and so do we at the church. Will you be our Sabbath school secretary, Marion? We really need you."

The love and concern in the pastor's voice melted Marion's rebellious pride. Tears filled her eyes and overflowed down her cheeks. She hadn't even planned to go back to church, but her will to resist fled in the face of such unconditional acceptance. "All right," she choked, "I'll do it. Thank you so much, pastor. Mother said you were praying for me all the time I was missing. I'm sure your prayers kept us from harm, hitchhiking and all. Now what does a Sabbath school secretary do?"

Elder Pike gave Marion some books and papers and explained the job a bit, had prayer with her, and left. Before his car was hardly out of the driveway, Marion flew into the kitchen and threw her arms around Cora's neck. "Oh, Mother, I'm sorry I ran away. And I'm sorry I said I didn't want to live with you. I didn't mean it. You've been so good to me ever since you adopted me, and I love you and Dad very much. I'm sorry I hurt you. Can you forgive me?"

As this was definitely one of those special times, Cora took her weeping daughter into her arms and wept too.

That night the family talked things over together.

"I know I could go to Union Springs Academy," Marion said, "but I really don't think I'm ready for boarding school yet. Besides, Stephanie might go there, and I don't want to be where she is right now. I know you don't want me in public school, Mom. Why can't I just stay home and work to make money for next year? Aunt Blanche could probably get me a job in the insurance company. I'm 16 now, you know. I'd really rather forget school this term, if you'd let me. I promise I'll go to South Lancaster next year if they'll take me back."

Andy thought the plan a sensible one, and Cora finally agreed—with one stipulation. From her salary, Marion must pay a weekly fee for room and board. The girl agreed, but secretly felt hurt that her mother would require such a thing. *There are times when I wonder if Mother really thinks of me as her daughter*, Marion thought that night. *You don't charge your own kids room and board!*

With the help of Aunt Blanche, Marion found a job as a file clerk at the insurance agency. So diligently did she work that she soon received one raise and then another, making Cora and Andy very proud of her. Cora felt sure of the change in Marion when she began bringing home a little gift each week for her adopted mother—her favorite Mary Oliver candies or cream cheese and walnut spread.

That year at home, Marion became better acquainted with her real mother, Dorothy, through her 19-year-old brother, Chuck. Frequently on leave from the naval shipyard in Boston, Chuck would drop by the insurance office in Hartford and take Marion to lunch. She often plied him with questions about their mother and father, and one day Chuck suggested that she visit their mother at her apartment in Hartford.

Marion hesitated. "I'm not sure she wants to see me, Chuck. When I ran away, Mother said that she'd asked Dorothy to take me back, and Dorothy didn't want me. I'd feel kind of funny going to see her."

Chuck shook his head. "You've got her all wrong. She's always said that she wanted you back but that she felt the Holmbergs could give you more than she ever could. She's had all she could do to support herself and me until I joined the Navy. At least now she has only herself to worry about. I'm sure she'd be glad to see you, Marion. Let me arrange it?"

Reluctantly Marion agreed, mentally promising herself that she would keep the meeting in perspective and not be at all upset if it fell through.

When the day arrived, however, her stomach cramped and her palms perspired. She hadn't seen her real mother for several years. What if Dorothy didn't like her? What if she actually hated her daughter? Could she—Marion—handle that?

Chuck picked her up at the office and took her to Dorothy's apartment for dinner. Equally nervous about the encounter, Dorothy had saved ration stamps for weeks to be able to buy the best of steak for Marion's meal with her. To her embarrassment—and Marion's—the girl wouldn't touch it.

"I'm sorry, but I just can't eat meat anymore," Marion apologized. "I've been a vegetarian for the past six years, and I think I'd get sick if I ate meat again. I'm really sorry. Can I just have potatoes and vegetables?"

When the evening ended, both Marion and Dorothy felt relieved. Neither had been truly comfortable in the other's presence. Too much had happened during the years they were apart. Feeling awkward, Dorothy didn't even give her daughter a goodbye hug. Puzzled, Chuck took her back to the Holmbergs, where she obviously felt more at ease.

That night Marion lay in bed wondering. All her life it seemed she had wanted someone to hold her hand, to give her a hug, to say "I love you." In her memory, no one before Cora ever had, and Cora's displays of affection were few and far between. Now she even felt awkward with her real mother. Would she ever find warm, accepting, unqualified love anywhere?

CHAPTER

5

Having been raised as an only child, Marion delighted in her new relationship with her brother, Chuck. Not only did he stop by the office to see her, but he began visiting her at Holmbergs' as well. Cora wasn't too pleased with this, for the young sailor certainly wasn't a Christian. She sensed, however, that her daughter was seeking her roots and wisely left her alone.

One evening Chuck showed up with a friend. "This is my good buddy, Bob," he announced. "Bob, meet my little sister, Marion."

Bob looked at the young lady with such obvious interest that it made her blush. A career Navy man from New York, Bob had a way with women—his wit and charm made up for his short, slender frame.

Bob let out a low whistle. "Wow! Why didn't you tell me you had such a good-looking sister? Have you entered her in the Miss America contest?"

Marion laughed. "You've been out to sea too long. I wouldn't even qualify for local potato queen! But anyway, glad to meet you. Would you fellows like some homemade apple pie? I just happened to bake one."

The sailors grinned and nodded in unison. "You bet!" Chuck said. "Navy grub is awful. A rat got into the kitchen the other day and died from it!"

Everyone laughed and headed for the kitchen, where Marion watched the hungry fellows devour her whole pie, one piece at a time. When they left, she thought she'd never met anyone so attractive as Bob. Mature, (26, Chuck said), worldly-wise, and every bit as quick-witted as she was, he seemed to offer the excitement and love she'd been looking for.

Before long he began picking her up at the office and driving her home. Then he started taking her to a movie before taking her home. Marion could hardly wait for the next date!

Although she always attended church and served as Sabbath school secretary, she still felt somewhat rebellious about religion. At work she took up smoking—a habit that was evident from the smell of her clothes and breath the very first day. Cora's heart sank, but instead of scolding her daughter, she fled to her bedroom to pray about the matter. Sometimes it seemed to her that Marion was doomed by her heritage to turn out wrong.

For several weeks Marion enjoyed Bob's attentions. Then one night he dropped a bombshell. "You know, kitten, I'm not getting any younger. You're so much fun to be with, and I think we make a perfect couple, don't you? I've always wanted to get married some day and have 10 children like my dad had. You grew up alone, so you have no idea how much fun that is. We used to get into more mischief!"

And for the next hour Bob regaled her with stories of his childhood. It sounded for all the world like *Cheaper by the Dozen*! Not yet 17, Marion had no intention of mothering one child, much less 10 of them, and she changed the subject quickly.

When Bob left that night, he was puzzled. For the first time, Marion made excuses when he said he'd pick her up from work the next day. Indeed, for the rest of the month, Marion put Bob off, breaking dates and avoiding him. Chuck took her to task. "Why are you treating Bob like this? You two seemed to be hitting it off so good and then—pow!—you turn into an icicle."

Marion sighed. "I'm just not ready to get married. He's nice and all that, but he's too serious. See if you can get him to back off, huh?"

When summer finally ended, Marion felt glad to escape to academy and get away from Bob, so attractive but too demanding. Where to go for academy posed another problem, however. Union Springs, where her past was unknown? Or back to South Lancaster Academy, where her friends were? The decision was made, oddly enough, by her cousin Roger from across the street.

Roger's mother had died, and Cora with her usual good-heartedness began to mother the teenager. Several times a week she invited her brother and his son to meals. Roger soon began looking to her to sew on his buttons and give him advice. As she talked with her nephew, Cora constantly pointed him to his heavenly Father for help in coping with the problems of life. Before long he was attending church with her and Marion.

No sooner had he been baptized than Cora began talking about academy. The whole thing sounded scary to him. "What's it like up there?" he asked Marion. "The rules must be really bad to have made you run away."

Marion laughed. "I didn't hate the rules, Roger. Stephanie did. I just felt rebellious in general and ran off because it was what I wasn't supposed to do. I wouldn't mind going back there if I didn't have to face all the people who know."

"I wouldn't mind going up there if *you* went," Roger hinted none too subtly. "At least then I'd know somebody. Why don't you go back to South Lancaster too? You can introduce me to all the pretty girls, and I'll pick out some swell fellows for you. How about it?"

Cora's voice interrupted from the kitchen. "You two are

going to school for an education, remember? Forget this boy/girl stuff for a few years."

The cousins laughed.

"How old were you when you got married?" Roger countered, his eyes twinkling. "It seems to me I heard you were only 17!"

"That's neither here nor there," Cora retorted. "You two just stick to your education. That's my advice."

All during August Roger pleaded with Marion, and at last she agreed to try South Lancaster Academy again. Cora talked to the principal, L. G. Sevrens, who consented to admit the girl on probation for the first quarter. The academy honored that commitment, even after they received her application blank, on which she truthfully admitted that she had last smoked a cigarette just the week before!

In September Marion and Roger jammed their belongings into the big old Packard for another trip to Massachusetts. During her year at home, the Lord had been working on Marion's heart despite her apparently contrary actions. As she left Hartford she determined that this time she would do well in school, obey the rules, get closer to the Lord, and (to ensure all this), have nothing to do with boys at all! Breaking up with Bob had been difficult.

Going back proved harder than Marion had imagined. Talk of her runaway buzzed around campus all fall, and everyone badgered her for details. She stuck to her resolutions, however, and continued to study and ignore the gossip and boys. Her resolve lasted until April.

Roger had about given up finding her a boyfriend when she finally accepted a date with one of his friends. All first semester she gave the cold shoulder to every guy he introduced to her. The date she finally accepted nearly renewed her resolve, however, for the fellow seemed obsessed with the runaway episode. In a Christian school why couldn't people be more considerate? She was ashamed of the past and wanted to forget it.

Summer came, long and lazy, and Marion felt exhausted from the emotional and mental stresses she'd faced all year. To her surprise, Cora and Andy urged her to take two months off and relax.

"But I'll need to make money for next year's tuition," Marion protested.

Cora smiled proudly. "That won't be necessary. I saved your room and board money from last summer. It's all put away for your school fees, so you can take a vacation!"

Shame turned Marion's face scarlet. How could she have thought her mother was greedy when she had asked for board money? Here she'd been planning ahead for her education. What a dear!

Back at SLA that fall, Marion felt happier and more relaxed. No one questioned her about running away anymore, and the teachers seemed to have confidence in her abilities in the classroom. She dated occasionally, but showed no interest in anyone in particular until second semester when Ed Hutchinson came on the scene.

Ed, the oldest child of a New Hampshire farm family of five children, had just returned from the war. During his Army years he had been based near Assam, India. Now back at college and older than the other students in his class, he already knew that he wanted to become a missionary and return to India. All he needed was an education and a wife to go with him.

Ed's sister, who had been attending occasional Friday night meetings at the college, noticed Marion and told Ed about her. "Ed, there's a girl you ought to meet. She's a little blonde from somewhere near Hartford, and she looks a lot like that Susan Cates you used to date. I know you'd like her."

Ed looked thoughtful. "Point her out to me sometime,

Sis," he said. "After all that time in the army, most girls look good to me!"

As soon as he saw her, Ed determined to meet Marion. When his buddy, Chris, asked to borrow his car so that he could cruise around and impress a girl named Marion, Ed refused to loan it. "I'm after that one myself," he told Chris. "Lay off."

That evening Ed drove over by the ball field, where Marion stood by the fence with a girlfriend, cheering the players. Impulsively he honked the horn. Marion's eyes never left the field. He honked again.

"I think the guy in that car is honking at you," Marion's girlfriend said.

"Maybe so," replied Marion, "but I don't intend to look at him. Any guy who wants to get acquainted with me better do more than drive around blowing his horn!"

That night Ed saw his sister. "That blonde you wanted me to meet is a snooty thing," he complained. "She wouldn't give me the time of day."

"What did you say to her?" his sister asked.

"Nothing," said Ed disgustedly. "I didn't speak to her at all. I just honked the horn, but she wouldn't even turn and look. How could I speak to her?"

Virginia laughed. "I don't blame her a bit. I don't look at fellows who honk, either. Why don't you try a different approach? I hear she's really a nice girl."

But Ed had his pride and didn't intend to cater to any female's whims. He dated others who were easier to get. Still, it rankled him that that "dumb little blonde" ignored him.

In May Ed drove over to New England Sanitarium and Hospital to visit an old girlfriend. In the lobby he was surprised to find the assistant girls' dean.

"Hello, Miss Tatum," he said. "What brings you over here?"

"Why, hi Ed. I brought one of my girls in for surgery

yesterday. Emergency appendectomy. I just came to check on her."

"Who is it?"

"Marion Holmberg, one of the academy juniors. You college kids probably don't know her. Want to go up with me to see her?"

"Sure," Ed replied, a strange look on his face. "Poor kid probably feels lonesome."

So Ed finally met Marion—under the supervision of the assistant dean! Determined to follow up his opportunity, he returned the next day with flowers—and the next and the next.

"Why are you here so much, Ed?" Marion asked. "I love having company, but it's not like South Lancaster is right around the corner. It must be 40 miles one way!"

"I'm making arrangements for some surgery for my mom," Ed replied, "and thought I might as well drop by since I was here anyway."

After Ed's fourth visit, Marion became definitely suspicious. How could it take so long to arrange a surgery when hers had been done within an hour of her admittance to the hospital? Ed must be up to something. After another week of daily visits, she was *sure* of it!

Marion's recovery was slow and full of setbacks. With only two weeks of the school year left, the doctor advised her to return home to recuperate. She refused.

"I've got to pass now so I can graduate next year," she insisted. "I have to take my finals. I'll go easy. Really I will."

Reluctantly the doctor consented to let her return to school provided someone would carry her up and down steps. Marion returned to school—but stubbornly refused to let anyone carry her—even when Ed Hutchinson offered!

After tests, Marion went home to rest, but returned to South Lancaster in a few weeks for camp meeting. She told her mother she wanted to see all her friends.

"She wants to see that Ed Hutchinson," Roger told Cora. "He's an older college guy who's already been in the Army and out again. I don't see what she sees in him. I introduced her to some really swell academy guys, and she paid no attention to them."

Still, Cora approved of camp meeting, so she let Marion go with friends. As Roger had predicted, she met and dated Ed Hutchinson several times. When she left, he took her address and said he might stop by during the summer on his way back from visiting a girlfriend in Washington, D.C. At that news, Marion's heart sank, for she had found Ed more fascinating than she cared to admit.

A few weeks later Ed and his friend Chris pulled up in front of the house. Cora opened the door, eyed both boys, and having heard all about Ed said silently, *Please Lord, let him be the tall one!* He was.

Inviting them in, she asked if they'd care to stay for supper. They accepted quickly.

Marion, dressed purposely in neat white shorts, came downstairs. Never having seen her like this at school, both fellows did a double take. What legs! Ed dropped his eyes politely, but Chris stared in frank appreciation. Ed fidgeted in his chair, crossing and uncrossing his legs, while Marion, oblivious to the excitement, strode back and forth setting the table.

At last he could stand it no longer. On the pretext of getting a drink of water, Ed followed her to the kitchen. "What on earth is wrong with you, Marion," he whispered. "Those pants are too short and too tight. Chris can't take his eyes off you, and I don't like it. Would you please go upstairs and get a skirt on?"

Marion stood as tall as her five-foot frame would allow, prepared to register her protest. Then she looked up at Ed towering over her and changed both her mind and then her clothes. Pleasing this guy was somehow very important to her. The incident did not escape Cora's notice, and Ed went up several notches in her estimation.

After supper Cora managed to keep Chris talking in the dining room so that Marion and Ed could spend a few minutes alone on the porch. Casually Ed informed her that he had broken up with the girl in D.C. He was headed home to help his dad with the summer farm work, but he'd sure like to see her—Marion—again sometime during vacation—if she didn't mind.

"May I wear my shorts?" she teased.

"Only if I come alone," he replied grimly. "And you be a good girl while I'm gone!"

After the fellows left, Marion chuckled. Who did Ed think he was, ordering her around? Still, she kind of liked him.

By the end of summer, Ed had given her his picture signed "All my love always" and was talking about "when we get married." Marion kept quiet, neither agreeing nor disagreeing.

Back at school in the fall, however, the two began dating in earnest. Since Marion was a high school senior and Ed a college sophomore, dating was difficult. At last Ed discovered that if he drove to the center of the campus and parked, Marion had to pass his car to get to her first class in the morning and would stop and talk to him. It was such a regular thing that the principal, Elder Chester Kellogg, became concerned.

Coming upon them one morning, he rapped on the fender to get their attention. "Ahem! Could I interrupt? There have been some complaints about you two visiting here every morning. Some of the faculty feel that this doesn't look too good. You're right out here in the middle of the campus, you know, and it's rather a public place to do your courting. If you must meet, I'd be glad to let you use my office once a week. But let's stop this daily rendezvous. OK?"

They agreed—but never did use Elder Kellogg's office.

Instead, they met other places, occasionally at the home of Ed's sister Virginia for Sabbath dinner.

By April it had been settled that Marion would marry Ed after graduation. She wasn't quite sure how it came about, as he never formally asked, but she knew she loved him. He was so clever, so masterful, so mature. True, he was like the rest of his New England family when it came to demonstrations of affection, but she soon learned that a chuck under the chin or a rumpling of the hair meant endearment to Ed. He didn't think all the mushy words and pawing around were necessary. To Marion, however, even that showed how grown-up he was—unlike the academy guys who couldn't keep their hands to themselves.

Marion knew she loved Ed, and she began looking forward to their marriage. Cora and Andy heartily agreed to hand over their daughter to the big, quiet New Englander. They were sure their girl would make a good farmer's wife.

CHAPTER

6

Two weeks after graduation, Cora helped Marion pack her clothes.

"I can hardly stand not being at your wedding," Cora said, trying to hold back the tears, "but your dad's been awfully sick, and I'm afraid to let him travel. I can't leave him alone, either. Oh, I do hope you're happy, dear. I feel sure the Lord brought you and Ed together."

Marion hugged her mother reassuringly. "I'm sure He did, Mother, and don't worry about not being at the wedding. Ed's folks can't come either. His mom is still recovering from her surgery. We don't have a thing planned, really. There's no money for a big affair, and Ed doesn't care much for 'fancy shindigs' as he calls them. We're just getting married in his pastor's living room."

Ed loaded her cedar chest and suitcases into his car, and the young couple headed for New Hampshire. Marion carefully hid her disappointment. She, like most girls, *did* like fancy weddings, but since neither family had much money, and they both planned to go to college, she realized that Ed's suggestion was really more practical.

In a light blue dress and white graduation shoes, Marion looked radiant. As a special treat, Ed had paid to get her beauty parlor permanent, and she felt—and looked—lovely. In Derry they stopped to pick up Ed's brother Malcolm and his sister Shirley for witnesses. On the way to the wedding, Malcolm asked where Marion's flowers were.

Ed groaned. "I never even thought of that!"

Malcolm grinned at Shirley and shook his head. How typical! Ed just wasn't romantic. Flowers to him weren't that necessary.

Marion didn't intend to let a little thing like flowers ruin her wedding. "I saw a flower shop on the way into town, honey," she told Ed. "Let's go back and see if we can get some talisman roses. They're my favorites."

Turning around, the wedding party hurried back to the shop and waited impatiently while the florist whipped together a bridal bouquet. Then they hastened on to the minister's house.

After a simple ceremony, Marion and Ed drove to Malcolm's home in Vermont, where his wife had prepared a reception for the newlyweds. There they visited with relatives for an hour or two and then left for a two-day honeymoon in Canada.

Upon their return, they moved into a small apartment above Ed's parents' home so that he could help his dad with the farm work and a new trucking business. The young folks planned to commute the 50 miles to Atlantic Union College, where Marion would take a three-year secretarial course and Ed theology. Marion figured that since they hadn't walked down the aisle together for a wedding, they'd make up for it by walking down the graduation aisle together.

The plan worked well first semester. Then Marion became pregnant. Second semester she dropped out of school. The birth of Mary Ellen, a lively baby, brought a great deal of pleasure to her parents and to both sets of grandparents.

Since Andy was feeling better these days, he and Cora came to visit the couple every few months and to bring them fresh garden produce. The old folks would sit on the couch as they passed Mary Ellen back and forth between them, marveling at her smile, her features, and her quick responses.

Between farm work and college requirements, Ed had very little time for the family and hardly any for sleep. He drove himself hard—working, trucking, commuting, and studying. The rest of that year time dragged for Marion, however—especially when Mary Ellen was sleeping. The young housewife missed the whirl of the campus activities that she had loved. Between Ed's exhaustion and the baby's needs, she seldom attended programs at South Lancaster. When she'd ask Ed to take her, he'd usually reply, "Oh, not tonight, Marion. I'm just too tired."

In an attempt to foster some social life, she invited the minister and his wife to Sabbath dinner. She had heard that they liked lentils, so she cooked up a big batch of the legumes with onions and tomatoes. As she took them from the stove, she smiled.

"These sure smell good," she told Mary Ellen. "I hope everyone likes them. With homemade bread, salad, and brownies for dessert, we'll have a nice Sabbath lunch."

As Mary Ellen banged her spoon on her high chair, Marion turned to smile at her. Suddenly the dish slipped from her hands and crashed to the floor. Lentils flew in all directions, showering mother, daughter, and the combination kitchen-dining room. Marion let out a wail.

"*My dinner!* What will I feed the pastor?"

Startled, Mary Ellen began howling, whether from hot lentils or surprise, her mother couldn't tell. She wiped off the baby and noted that the dish itself had landed upright and that more than half of the contents remained inside. She retrieved it thankfully and began cleaning up the apartment.

For a week afterward she found lentils in the most unusual places—under couch cushions, inside the overhead light fixture, and under the doormat, but her guests never had any idea of what had gone on before their arrival. They complimented Ed on his lovely family and told Marion what a good cook she was.

Ed agreed with their sentiments. He had known that all along. Her baked goods were outstanding, and when she made rich, fat brownies stuffed with nuts and then topped them with thick whipped cream skimmed from the dairy crocks, he licked his lips and sighed. "These are so good I could eat them every day," he declared. "You sure know how to make brownies."

Pleased at the unaccustomed praise, Marion began making her special brownies every Friday as a Sabbath treat. Ed gobbled them down and took seconds. Every Friday for an entire year Marion labored to produce the delicacy for her hardworking husband.

Then one Friday night, Ed pushed back his chair. "That's it!" he declared. "I've had enough! I've had brownies until they're running out my ears. I don't want to see another for at least a decade!"

Marion drew back in astonishment then burst out laughing. "You said you thought you could eat them every day," she teased. "Sorry I overdid it. You kept taking seconds, so I had no idea you were tired of them. I'll stop. Why didn't you say anything before?"

While the episode amused them both, Marion did wish that Ed hadn't waited a year to tell her. On the other hand, she realized that his New England parents didn't communicate well either, so he came by the trait honestly.

In the years that followed, Ed graduated from college, but his dad's failing health kept the young couple from leaving the farm. The arrival of a second child, Alice, was a welcome diversion from farm routine. While Ed milked cows and ran the tractor, he still dreamed of returning to India, not with the U.S. Army, but with the army of the Lord. Yet the dream seemed impossible.

Then Elder Lange met them. He was on furlough from

India and had met Ed when the young man was a soldier in Assam. He had encouraged Ed then to come back to India, and now he urged the couple again to apply for mission service. His tales of India fascinated them. When they applied, but received no response, Ed concluded that perhaps the Lord didn't want them in the mission field.

Meanwhile, he received a call to Mt. Aetna Academy in Maryland. The terms were not attractive. For half of what they were now earning on the farm, Ed would teach seventh and eighth grades at the church school, industrial arts at the academy, and keep the school's two buses in working order! However, despite these drawbacks and the fact that she was seven months pregnant again, Marion favored taking the call. She was weary of farm life and hoped that in a new location Ed could work less and see more of her and the girls. Besides, Marion ached for her very own home—not her mother-in-law's!

The beginning of the school year found them in a small, rented house near Mt. Aetna. Rumor had it that the place had been built over a rattlesnake den, and Marion hated going into the dark basement to wash clothes, which was quite often as the diaper pail seemed to refill automatically. With the move, her pregnancy, and two preschoolers, Marion stayed super busy. Fortunately, the house sat in an isolated section backed by woods, so the children had ample place to play without danger. At least that was true until the convict escaped.

Radio alerts warned the community that a dangerous criminal had escaped from a nearby prison. All the neighbor women were alarmed. Marion was especially nervous because Ed spent nearly every evening repairing the school buses, leaving her alone with the two girls. One afternoon when the staff ladies came to give her a surprise baby shower, they scrutinized the area carefully before climbing out of their cars—and shortened the party in order to get back to more

57

populated areas before it got too dark.

After an anxiety-filled week, police apprehended the criminal within sight of Marion's front door. He had been hiding in the woods and stealing food from the kitchen in an unopened youth camp in the vicinity. Upon his capture, the entire community breathed a collective sigh of relief.

That October Ann arrived to complete the Hutchinson family. Alice and Mary Ellen loved helping with the baby, and keeping up with all three of them occupied Marion completely. At the end of the school year, the whole family moved back to New Hampshire so that Ed could help his father with the farming during the summer.

One morning as Marion scurried around the house to clean up breakfast dishes, she heard a knock at the door. Opening it, she nearly fainted with shock. Her real mother, Dorothy, whom she had not seen since academy days, was standing on the porch. After an awkward moment, Marion invited her inside.

"Mother Dorothy! What on earth brought you up here?" she asked. "I haven't seen you in years."

"I know," Dorothy said. "I'm sorry. I can never decide if you're better off left alone or if I should keep in touch with you. You seemed so close to the Holmbergs, and since I had signed papers making you legally theirs, it didn't seem quite right to keep interfering in your life.

"But when Grandma Holmes told me you had married Ed Hutchinson in Derry, New Hampshire, and that you now had three little girls, I just had to come and see you. Are you happy, Marion? Is Ed good to you?"

Alice and Mary Ellen stopped playing and stared curiously at the visitor. Marion drew Alice onto her lap and brushed back her curls. "Oh yes, Ed is very good to me, and the Lord has blessed me with three lovely daughters. Girls, I'd like you to meet your . . ." Marion's voice wavered uncertainly and stopped.

Sensing her discomfort, Dorothy came to her rescue. "Aunt Dorothy," she prompted. "Just call me Aunt Dorothy."

Marion heaved a sigh of relief. That title would avoid many unpleasant explanations, because as far as the children knew, Cora and Andy were Mommy's parents.

While Dorothy talked with the girls, Marion hurried to the bedroom and lifted Ann from her crib. Coming back to the living room, she laid the baby in Dorothy's arms. "This is Ann Delight," she announced.

Dorothy's eyes filled with tears as she buried her face in the baby's soft hair. All the years of longing for her own baby girl filled her with such a poignant regret she could hardly bear it. Only the years of patient discipline kept her from crying aloud for wasted love and lost time.

When Ed came in from the barn, Marion introduced him to "Aunt Dorothy," too, but he knew immediately who she was. Dorothy watched as he picked up baby Ann and threw her into the air, both of them laughing as he caught her on the way down.

"You have a beautiful family, Ed," Dorothy commented.

Ed smiled proudly, but in his New England fashion, he merely shrugged. "They'll do in a pinch," he said and went off to wash up.

At Dorothy's alarmed look, Marion leaned close to whisper, "It's OK, Mother Dorothy. He can't bring himself to say much, but he loves us a great deal. You know how New Englanders are sometimes!"

Dorothy laughed, relieved at the explanation, and during lunch she picked up reassuring little signs of his affection for the girls and Marion. After lunch Marion put the children down for a nap, asked Grandma Hutchinson to keep an eye on them, and took her mother for a ride into the country. Stopping by the rippling river, Marion began to talk. "All these years I have wanted to ask you something," she said.

"Why did you give me away? Didn't you love me?"

Dorothy looked horrified. "Love you? I *adored* you! You were the only little girl I had."

"Then why did you keep Chuck and give me away?" Marion asked fiercely. "You used to say you would get me back as soon as you could afford it, but you never did. You managed to keep Chuck, though. Why not me?"

Pain filled Dorothy's eyes. She looked out the car window at the flowing river. "It's a long story," she began, "but I'll try to explain.

"I met your father at a dance. He was handsome and charming but on the short side, so he picked me out of the crowd since I'm short too. We really hit it off that night, and he began calling on me regularly.

"I was living with my mother and her mother, Grandma Holmes. Charlie showered me with candy and flowers and was so much fun I fell head over heels for him. We were both awfully young, you know.

"So I married him, and before long Chuck arrived. By this time, your father had found a job in Hartford and was coming home only once a month, if that often. He was always chasing some impossible dream and hardly had enough to pay our rent and keep food in the house. With Chuck to care for and you on the way, I couldn't work, so I stayed home, believing what he told me—that he'd be back any day to move us all to Hartford.

"Because we were behind in the rent, when he did come home, he'd sneak in after dark to avoid the landlord. None of the neighbors ever knew he'd been to see us."

Dorothy sighed, remembering. "Those weekends were wonderful. He'd come with silly presents. He was always full of optimism and enthusiasm, and he'd charm both of us. Chuckie loved him and so did I.

"When my pregnancy began to show, however, my mother became most upset. 'What will the neighbors think?'

she demanded. 'Nobody knows Charles has been visiting you. There's been enough scandal in this family already with your own father running off when you were little. I can't stand any more. Why don't you get out of town until that baby arrives and then put it up for adoption? There's no way you can handle two kids, anyway.' "

Marion's face tightened as she listened. "You mean your mother thought people would think I was illegitimate?"

"That's right. So she sent me off to keep house for old Mr. Caine, who lived in a cabin back in the woods. I was supposed to get $5 a week plus room and board. He only paid me the first week, but I knew Mother didn't want me home, so I kept working.

"The last month of my pregnancy, though, he sent me to help his daughter, Lillian, who was having a baby. She had two in diapers, I had one, and I slept on a horrible cot in the hall and did her housework.

"She had the baby at home, as many women did in those days, and when I was helping the doctor deliver it, he turned to me, eyed my stomach, and said, 'Good grief, girl, you ought to be in this bed, too!' Let me tell you, I agreed wholeheartedly, but I kept working until you came.

"At the hospital I hoped Charlie would show up. He'd always promised that when I had my baby, he'd be there and take us all to Hartford. He'd been there when Chuckie was born. But even though I sent word to his parents and letters to him, he never showed."

Dorothy's voice faltered and stopped, her face reflecting remembered pain.

"Go on, Mother. What happened?"

"Well, the delivery was hard. I had to stay in the hospital for three days. When they discharged me, I was so sick and exhausted I could hardly see straight. Mother came and got us and put me right back in bed. In the morning, she called the social worker to come get you. I cried and begged, but it did no good.

" 'You can't manage this child,' she declared, 'and I certainly can't support grandma and you and *two* children. She'll get good care at the Home, Dorothy. Be sensible! I don't want the neighbors gossiping, and you can't manage two children. This one's going to the Home.'

"What could I do? I was so sick I couldn't take care of myself, much less you children. Your father's parents loved Chuckie, so when I went to the hospital to have you, they took him and just kept him. Of course I was sick a lot then. I was coming down with tuberculosis but didn't know it. So you went to the Home.

"When I got on my feet again, I got a job at the dime store as a clerk, and I'd save my lunch money to have trolley fare to go and see you on Sundays.

"I'd rock you and sing to you—you were so beautiful with your blonde hair and blue eyes. Everyone remarked how smart you were too."

Marion looked away uncomfortably as her mother's voice broke again. "You have no idea how I wanted you back. I just couldn't manage it. Then they moved you to Mrs. McGraw's place. She kept half a dozen babies. At first I thought you were getting good care there, but then I began to wonder why you were sleeping every time I went. I asked the social service to investigate, and they found her giving all the babies paregoric to keep them quiet! I could have killed her! Imagine a woman drugging babies like that!"

Marion was beginning to understand. "I'd be furious if anyone did that to my kids," she agreed. "I'm sorry, Mother. I had no idea you'd had such a hard time. Grandma Holmes tried to tell me about my background, but Aunt Essie got mad and stopped her. I've always wondered what she wanted to say. Now I think I know."

Dorothy's handkerchief twisted in knots as her hands

wrung it nervously, but she continued. "Then you went to Mrs. Johnson's. She was really a wonderful woman, motherly and loving. I visited you there every chance I got. My sister Harriet went, too, and bought you the cutest little snowsuit. You were darling! Unfortunately, Mrs. Johnson got TB and had to go to the sanatorium. That's when you were moved to the Litches' place.

"By that time I was sick myself, coughing and spitting up blood. They diagnosed tuberculosis and sent me to the sanatorium. The doctor said I might live a year. By that time, I really didn't care. I wanted to die. Both my children had been taken from me, I had divorced Charles for desertion, and my mother just fussed about what an expense my illness was. What did I have to live for?

"Somehow, though, I kept on living. When the social worker came to the hospital to talk to me about letting the Holmbergs adopt you, the Lord knows I didn't want to. But I tried to do what was best for you, Marion." Dorothy choked back tears.

"*My* life was already messed up. Holmbergs were friends of Grandma Holmes, you know, and she'd told them about you. It wasn't as if you were going to strangers.

"When the social worker told me that Cora felt the Lord had sent you to her, I knew that they were godly people and would raise you right. Since I expected to die any time, I signed the adoption papers. It was the hardest thing I ever did. I cried all night, but I did it."

Slowly the truth dawned in Marion's mind. Dorothy hadn't deserted her. Now that she had babies of her own, Marion could understand better how frantic her mother must have felt. She reached for Dorothy's trembling hand and held it. "It's OK," she said softly. "I understand now. I'm so glad you told me what really happened. Holmbergs didn't want to talk about it, and Grandma Holmes wasn't allowed to. For years I've felt that I wasn't wanted, wasn't loved.

"When Father came to Holmbergs' to see me that time, I wouldn't even see him. I hated him. He'd left us. The Litches' kids and kids at school teased me to death about not having a father. I'd pretend he was coming, and they'd laugh when he didn't show up."

"Oh, my dear," her mother said, tears streaming down her face. "I did the best I knew for you. What else could I have done?"

Marion shook her head. "Nothing. But I'm glad you came now—really glad. Could I ask you one more question, though? When you did get out of the hospital, why did you take Chuck back and not me?"

The older woman wiped her eyes. "You were receiving love and care in a good home. Grandma Brainard was getting too old to look after a boy of Chuck's age. She couldn't keep up with him, and he was getting away with everything. I didn't want him to be irresponsible like his father, so as soon as I could get my own job and apartment, I brought him to live with me. I still couldn't support two children, though. I barely made it with Chuck.

"And I suppose you wonder why I didn't come to see you at Holmbergs' more often, don't you?"

Marion nodded.

"The social worker told me that since Holmbergs had adopted you, it would be best if I stayed away so you'd relate to them and mind what they told you. Children who have too many homes and too many options, she said, become upset and restless. So many times I longed to see you, but I stayed away. I wanted you to have the best possible chance for a good life.

"I did go secretly to the hospital when you went in for that tonsillectomy, though. I'm not sure you knew I was there, but when I heard you were sick, I couldn't stay away. I had to see you. I sat by you until you came out from under the anesthetic."

Marion shook her head in amazement. "I never knew you were there!"

"I didn't think you did. But I kept track of you. I was glad Chuck brought you to see me in Hartford, but by then we seemed like strangers. I guess we still are, but now that you're married and all, do you think we could get to know each other a little better? Ann looks so much like you did. I'd love to see you and the children occasionally. We've missed so much already.

"Of course, if you feel I'd just mess up your life again, I'll bow out. I really want what's best for you, but I wish we could get to know each other."

Marion reached for her mother's other hand and held them both. "I want to know you, too, Mother Dorothy. For all these years I've been afraid I was so ugly or bratty you couldn't stand to keep me. Or maybe I was too much like my father. I guess you did the best you could, and Holmbergs have certainly been good to me. If it weren't for them, I wouldn't have come to know the Lord or to have met Ed, and I can't imagine life without either.

"We've applied to go overseas, though, as missionaries. Did you know? But even if we do, you can write and I'll answer. I do want you to be part of my life."

Leaving the river, Marion drove her mother to the train station so she could get back to Hartford for the next day's work. Brief as it was, that conversation put to rest many of Marion's old fears and insecurities and proved to be the start of a real friendship between a young woman and her mother.

CHAPTER

7

As if the Lord had been waiting until Marion's mind was more at peace, the Hutchinsons received a call from the General Conference soon after Dorothy's visit. "We're wondering, Brother Hutchinson, if you are still interested in mission service. Our records show that you refused one call, but perhaps you'd be interested in another."

Ed listened in astonishment. "I never *received* any overseas call," he protested. "I've wanted to go back to Assam ever since I was in India with the Army. Yes, we're definitely interested."

During the next few months, the young couple received two calls—one to Assam in northwest India and the other to Falakata in the northeast. They opted for the first and filled out visa applications. To their dismay, visas were denied. Records showed that Ed had been in Assam during the war. Perhaps he was now returning as a U.S. spy! Later applications for visas to Falakata were also denied due to the political situation there.

Grandpa Hutchinson was greatly disappointed. Realizing that he could never manage the farm without Ed but longing to see his son become an overseas missionary, Grandpa had sold off the farm's herd of cows as soon as the first mission call came. Now it seemed a wasted gesture. The whole family continued to pray earnestly for guidance.

When it seemed they were not leaving the States, Ed and Marion accepted a call to Barclay, Maryland, where Ed would be principal and teacher in the Moffit School.

That spring, however, they were invited to go to Pakistan. "After all," the brethren argued, "Pakistan was formerly part of India and the cultures are much the same. We're sure you'd do well as teacher and assistant principal at Pakistan Union High School."

The young couple agreed, and this time visas were granted. As if to celebrate the culmination of their dreams, the sailing date was set for a holiday—the Fourth of July, 1957. It seemed to Marion and Ed that their departure for the mission field occasioned more family concern than any other event thus far in their lives. Both sets of parents, several of Ed's brothers and sisters, and many friends stood on the New York dock as the *S.S. City of Bath* pulled away.

For once in her life, Marion felt hugged enough. Leaving her mother and father had been especially difficult because of Andy's poor health. What if she never again saw the only father she had ever known?

Even Ed seemed unusually moved by the parting. Holding Ann in one arm, he put the other around his wife. "Buck up, girl," he told her fondly. "We'll be back before you know it. Now let's get that cabin straightened up. I can hardly get in the door for all the luggage you brought!"

For 28 days the ship sailed nonstop toward Pakistan. By the second day Ed's restless exploration of the ship had revealed that it was transporting a new train on the bottom deck. But for safety reasons, passengers were confined to the crowded passenger deck.

Although she got used to the boat, Marion always kept an eye on the railing for fear that her girls might fall overboard. Mary Ellen, now 9, tried to help her, but 6-year-old Alice had such an adventuresome spirit that she was hard to keep track of. And Ann, not quite 3, would go anywhere with anyone.

Since Mary Ellen had finished only half of third grade when they left the States, Marion hauled out the books and began helping her daughter complete the year. Two American children at the mission station in Pakistan would be in fourth grade the next year, and Marion hoped that Mary Ellen would fit into that class in the little overseas school.

For once Ed had no cows to milk, no bus to repair, and no trucks to drive, so the family basked in his undivided attention. Feeling more like a woman than a mother for once, Marion delighted in dining at the captain's table with Ed—minus the children, who were taken by the stewardess to an early dinner. The slow, relaxed shipboard pace was just what Marion needed after all her frantic packing and scurrying around.

By the end of the month, however, everyone was eager to be on land again, and Ed was more than eager to get back to work. Raised by a farmer who felt work and life were inseparable, Ed had a hard time resting.

The seaport of Karachi, Pakistan, boggled Marion's mind. Ed had seen Asia already and took it in stride, but Marion and the girls stared in amazement at horse-drawn Victorian carriages and camel carts pulling heavy loads. Everything seemed to be mass confusion.

"Where's that fellow going with our suitcases, Ed?" Marion called anxiously.

Ed turned his head just in time to see his luggage disappearing down the gangplank. He ran after it. "Hey, those are mine!" he shouted. "Who told you to move them?"

The coolie stopped, smiled, babbled in Urdu, and waited.

"Put them back on deck," Ed said, gesturing plainly. "We're waiting for an American to come for us."

Shrugging, the man hauled the suitcases back up the gangplank, set them with the other luggage, and vanished.

"Good thing you saw that, Stub," Ed said, using his pet name for his short wife. "Isn't this great?"

Marion grimaced. "It might be if someone would come to get us. Oh look! There's Bob Reynolds, the missionary we met at the General Conference!"

Before long the Hutchinsons and their luggage were in the Karachi Seventh-day Adventist Hospital van for a breathtaking ride through the city. At every intersection Marion braced herself for a crash. Donkeys, bicycles, three-wheeled taxis, regular taxis, camels, and oxcarts all vied for a piece of the road. No one seemed to follow any driving rules. Red lights meant little, and yellow lights nothing!

Elder Reynolds whipped in and out of traffic with ease, frequently taking his eyes off the road to explain things to his passengers. "This is the local market," he said, pointing to a large covered area. "We buy most of our produce here. And those vendors over there are selling fresh lemonade. See all the lemons inside the big block of ice? It looks delicious—but it's instant diarrhea if you drink it.

"That fellow there is making jalabies. They're a pretzel-shaped fried sweet that's really good. Safe to eat if you get them hot out of the oil, too."

Marion's head swam. She'd never remember all this. And that market! Where was the good old Safeway? Ed saw her worried look and reached over to give her hand a reassuring squeeze. She made a face at him. He knew what she was thinking, but he knew that somehow she'd cope. She was definitely a survivor.

The following days blurred together. Marion kept the children in the hospital guest room while Ed negotiated the release of their household goods at the docks. After an incredibly dusty 24-hour train ride, they arrived in Lahore. There they crowded into a mission car sent to transport them the last 35 bumpy miles to Pakistan Union High School at Chuharkana, their destination.

Tired and dirty, they tumbled out of the car to be greeted by Mr. R. K. Hamilton, the principal. "Well, well," he boomed. "You finally made it. Looks like you've got a flock of little girls. Come on in for supper. Marion, you're just in time to play the piano for prayer meeting. Want you to feel at home, you know, so we'll put you right to work."

Marion's heart sank! Play the *piano*? For *prayer meeting*? *Like this*? What a first impression she'd make! But after supper, the principal insisted, and Marion found herself pounding out "Sound the Battle Cry" on a terribly ancient, out-of-tune piano. As she played, her Brainard rebellion rose full force. *I'd like to sound a battle cry!* she thought fiercely. *If he does this to me again, there's going to be war!*

At the end of the meeting, the newcomers were called forward and seated on the platform. Trying to keep the children from fussing, Marion only half heard an elaborate English greeting and a seemingly endless Urdu welcoming song. The girls quieted as they watched the drummer beat the "tabla" and the harmonium player squeeze the bellows at the back of an accordion-like instrument.

At the end of the ceremony, students draped garlands of flowers and golden tinsel around the Hutchinsons' necks until they felt like Christmas trees. Although Ed appreciated the thought, he could hardly wait to get the perfumed decorations off. The children and Marion, however, thought the garlands delightful.

The next day Marion began settling into the small staff house to which they'd been assigned, while Ed was introduced to his new job of being assistant principal, math/science teacher, and equipment repairman.

Morning began with a bang. Literally! An explosion rocked the small mission house, and Marion grabbed the baby. "Get the girls!" she shouted to Ed.

Ed laughed. "Relax, Stub. It's just the puffing gun going off."

Later that day Mr. Hamilton took the family upstairs in the tall gray building behind their home and showed them the big metal cannon that exploded grain into puffed wheat. The girls held their hands over their ears while the deafening explosion again shook the campus as the gun was pointed down and pressure released. Puffed wheat flew from the gun's mouth into a huge screened room with a removal chute at the bottom. The principal scooped up a handful and gave it to Mary Ellen.

Tentatively she nibbled. "It's good," she announced. "Try it, Mama."

Since the others liked it, too, puffed wheat became a regular breakfast food at Marion's table.

With a background of New England thrift and make-do, Marion began creating a home. She talked Ed into putting shelves in a long, tall packing case, thus converting it into a linen "closet." Then she went to town with Ed to see what food she could find to fill the big kitchen cupboard.

Buying groceries in Lahore proved both fascinating and frustrating. Shortening was "vegetable ghee," a coarse grainy fat. Cornstarch was "corn flour"—a name Marion associated with blue blossoms. All lentils and beans were "dahl," and many of them were new to the American housewife.

She arrived home exhausted, put the children to bed, and began storing her purchases. Ed drove to the nearby cafeteria storeroom to unload the sacks of wheat he'd purchased in town that day.

Marion took her flour canister from the large cupboard, filled it, and started to replace it when a movement in the cupboard caught her eye. A frog? A lizard? Whatever it was, it frightened her, and she slammed the door shut with such force it bounced open again, revealing a snake's head, swinging back and forth. All Marion's childhood fears came flooding back, threatening to paralyze her. Instantly she slammed the door again, and jammed a chair against it.

Out of the house she flew and over to the cafeteria. "Ed!"

she screamed, "Come quick! There's a snake in my cupboard."

Used to his wife's nervousness over creepy things, he continued to unload the wheat. "Calm down, Stub. It was probably a lizard."

"It was *not*!" his wife gasped hysterically. "It was a snake. Oh, come quick! The girls are in bed, but what if they go to the kitchen for a drink?"

Albert, a student helping him with the wheat, spoke up. "Maybe we'd better go, Sahib. Sometimes we do have snakes."

Together the three trooped back to the house. Ed opened the cupboard with an expansive gesture and stared in horror at *two* snakes coiled and ready to strike. Quickly he slammed the door and held it shut.

"Run to the shed, Marion," he ordered, "and get those two new axe handles. Quick!"

Trembling at the thought of what might be out in the shed, Marion obeyed and returned with the weapons. Giving one to Albert and keeping the other for himself, Ed opened the cupboard doors gingerly.

"Get that one," he yelled, attacking the larger snake himself, and within minutes the two reptiles lay dead on the floor.

"Pitch them outside," he told Albert, heading for the door. "Then let's finish that wheat. Be back in a bit, Stub."

After the men were gone, Marion nearly tore the house apart looking for more snakes. Frantically she flipped up couch cushions, emptied the dirty clothes hamper, and awakened the children and ordered them out of their beds while she shook the covers. At last, satisfied that there were no more reptiles, she tucked her groggy girls back into bed and returned to the kitchen. After all, the groceries still had to be put away. This was one story she didn't intend to include in her letters to Cora and Andy.

Mary Ellen and Alice began attending the small overseas school, swelling the enrollment to seven. Marion had Mary Ellen now ready to join the others in fourth grade, but the young missionary was completely unprepared when Principal Hamilton informed her that the teacher was leaving, and she had been selected to take over the overseas church school.

"But I've had no teacher training," she protested, "and only one semester of college."

The principal smiled. "Out here you'll do a lot of things you have no training for," he informed her. "You just take the job and do the best you can."

After a night of rebellious tears, Marion began teaching the church school—seven wiggly kids in six grades. For the first two months, she cried every night, begging Ed to let her quit.

"I don't know what I'm doing," she wept, "and I'll mess these kids all up. Please make Hamilton assign this to somebody else."

Finally Ed wearied of the subject. "OK," he agreed, "just quit. Then everybody will know that my wife's a quitter."

"I'm *not* a quitter," she snapped, "and I wouldn't want to embarrass *you* for anything! Forget it. I'll keep teaching. But if the kids don't know anything when the year's over, don't blame me!"

Smoldering but determined, she returned the next day to the classroom. Wracking her brain to remember some of the teaching techniques she'd seen used at Hartford church school, she did a better job than usual. Before long she was covering all 35 subjects easily and even had time for extras to make school fun. When she went to Mr. Hamilton to ask him for craft paper and art supplies, he grinned. "Anything your little heart desires," he declared, signing her requisition form. "The kids are enjoying your classes so much. They say they never had a better teacher."

His commendation gave Marion more confidence in her

abilities, and as time passed, her natural teaching talent blossomed.

Meanwhile, Ed found his job more than time-filling, as usual. Used to working at farm chores until they were done, he now tried to stick with the campus repair and maintenance jobs until they were completed, too, a hopeless task. All hours of the day and night staff members called him to repair machinery or get the puffing gun's pressure regulated properly. Marion and the girls sometimes saw him at meals, but more often than not he turned up late and ate by himself. Under his supervision the campus soon began to improve, and the puffing industry increased its production and sales.

With Marion teaching, someone was needed around the house, so the Hutchinsons hired Rashim, the farm manager's wife, to cook, clean, and baby-sit. A mother herself, she had no trouble managing the three girls, especially the baby. Marion discovered, however, that Rashim did things a bit differently than she was used to. When she first found her sitting on the floor and kneading the bread in a pan, Marion began to protest. Then on second thought, she let Rashim alone. The pan was clean, Rashim was comfortable, and except for the fact that Westerners don't usually cook down on the floor, there really was no reason to change the procedure. It was simply a cultural difference.

The household ran smoothly until Rashim left to bear her ninth child! Then they hired Rahmet, a happy-go-lucky fellow with a personality all his own. The girls loved him, but Marion constantly worried that he was spoiling them. Although the older ones were supposed to make their beds (Marion believed firmly in teaching children to work), they could get out of it if they sneaked into the kitchen and whispered to Rahmet.

"I no want make bed this morning, Rahmet. You make, OK?"

Rahmet would grin. "OK," he'd whisper conspiratorially. "I make. Don't tell!" And the girls would skip out to play.

Sometimes he found it difficult to vacuum the rugs with Ann riding horseback on the sweeper's canister, but he never complained. "OK, Ann, you go now. OK?"

"No, Rahmet. Pull more. Ride horse. Pull, Rahmet."

And away they'd go across the living room, both giggling.

Rahmet loved "pahlties." Birthday "pahlties," anniversary "pahlties," any kind of "pahlties." As soon as he heard one was in the offing, he would take Marion's cookbooks and leaf through them, looking at the pictures.

"Let's make this one, Memsahib," he would say. "It look good. Nice and pretty. OK?"

"OK," Marion would reply. And Rahmet, guessing at the ingredients, usually came up with a reasonable facsimile. Most of his concoctions were even edible!

He loved fixing "subusketti" (spaghetti) and egg salad with "mig-a-nigs" (mayonnaise). Desserts were always "results" to him, and he became an expert at fixing eggplant parmigiana, which he called "eggplant Farmer John!" Rahmet kept everyone happy and did a good job with the cleaning and cooking. Without him, Marion could never have managed to teach and run the house too.

Each morning Rahmet headed for the market with a basket on his arm and came home with the day's fresh fruits and vegetables. Marion discovered that in order to have peas year round, she had to buy them in the pod in 80-pound lots during the one month they were available, hire women to shell them all day in the front yard, and then freeze them for future use. Squash and eggplant, however, grew year-round, and Marion became very adept at disguising them in order to get fresh vegetables into her family's menu.

During the winter, "kinnus" arrived. The delicious loose-skinned oranges came in hundred-pound sacks for about 80 cents! During the season the family drank all the fresh orange juice they could hold. The girls learned to love guavas and eat them right from the campus trees, green, with chili pepper and salt, just like their Pakistani playmates.

The large campus provided a safe playground for all the staff children, and they ran from one end of it to the other, balancing on the edges of irrigation ditches that crisscrossed the desert compound. Temperatures ranged from near freezing in the winter to 120 in the shade in midsummer. Electric fans hung from high ceilings on six-foot stems, stirring the hot air just enough to make the classrooms bearable.

At night everyone suffered with the heat. Dorm students dragged their rope-strung beds into the courtyard or onto the flat dormitory roofs for sleeping. After many sleepless nights, Ed managed to scrounge up an Army surplus air-conditioner and install it in the bedroom. It proved to be a double blessing—providing coolness while muffling the explosions of the puffing gun.

The Hutchinsons' home lacked many American amenities. The poured concrete floor contained so many potholes that in trying to drag her portable washer from the bathroom into the hall, Marion broke three of its legs! The house contained a single cold water faucet, but directly in front of the building stood an old fashioned hand pump, which spewed out cool water. On hot, dry days the girls loved to put on their bathing suits and play at the pump.

As tough as Ed was, he did love a hot shower. Wracking his brain for some way to manage it, he finally installed a large metal tank outside the bathroom wall. It hovered two feet off the ground, leaving room below for a fire. An opening in the top allowed the gardener to fill it with a hose. Getting a hot bath required some planning ahead, of course, but after the water had been heated over the wood fire for several hours, one could turn a faucet on the pipe that stuck through the bathroom wall and enjoy a hot shower.

Desert storms frequently blew across the campus and left

everyone with dust-covered furniture and gritty teeth. Whenever a dust storm began, all the occupants of the house flew into action, pulling the shutters closed and latching windows.

One night at the first shutter bang, Ed, Marion, and the girls ran to close the windows. Stepping gingerly over the curtains her mother had been sewing on the living room floor, Mary Ellen reached for the window.

"Ow!" she yelled. "Something stuck me!"

Latching the shutter, she raced back to her mother's bed and examined her foot.

"You probably stepped on a pin in my drapes," Marion decided. "You'll be OK in a minute."

But Mary Ellen's foot didn't get better. It throbbed and began to lose feeling. When the numbness started up Mary Ellen's leg, Marion ran to consult Mr. Hamilton.

"May be a scorpion," he said. "Let's get her to the doctor."

Ed scooped up his daughter and raced with her across the campus to the home of Dr. Carrie Robbins, who ran the school's dispensary. By the time they reached there, the child was numb to the waist.

"Yes, I think she's been stung by a scorpion," Dr. Robbins announced after examining Mary Ellen. "I'd better give her a shot of adrenaline and see if we can halt this reaction."

When Mary Ellen stabilized, Ed carried her home and the family began a hunt. With a stubborn set to her jaw, Marion began overturning every piece of furniture in the living room. Finding nothing there, she started in on the nearby bedroom.

"Ed! Come quick!" she shouted. "It's here under the trunk!"

Ed dashed in from the kitchen and dispatched an ugly three-inch scorpion.

"It's a good thing it didn't sting the baby," Dr. Robbins

commented the next day. "That much poison could have killed her."

Family worship that night was far from routine. Ed and Marion thanked God for sparing Mary Ellen's life and for Dr. Robbins' presence on campus. And tiny Ann ended her prayer right on target—"And don't let any bad bugs get us, Jesus. Amen."

With the hospital 35 miles away—an hour and a half by car—the college residents appreciated Dr. Robbins immensely. So did the neighboring villagers, who poured into the little dispensary in such numbers that the poor doctor could hardly get any rest. But even with expert medical help not every life could be saved. Marion learned how sudden death could be when one of the academy boys came down with violent diarrhea one morning and died the next afternoon. Nothing Dr. Robbins did could save him.

Because of the heat and lack of embalming facilities, the law required that the dead be buried within 24 hours of death. With no time to build a coffin and still conduct a burial before sundown, Ed dashed home.

"Marion, take the stuff out of that packing case we're using for a linen closet," he ordered. "I need it for a coffin."

Swiftly Marion emptied the cupboard, and Ed dragged it outside. Together he and the gardener carried it to the industrial workshop, where he pulled out the shelves he had carefully inserted a few months before. Then Marion and other staff wives lined it with white cloth and sprinkled it with perfume. Ed placed the body in the box.

Students and staff wept as the coffin was lowered into a hastily dug grave in the cemetery behind the farthest staff house. For Dr. Robbins the ceremony was especially painful. Her own husband lay in that graveyard, a victim of polio only a year before.

That night as they lay in bed, Marion felt a return of all her childhood insecurities. What would happen to her if Ed died suddenly like that? She reached out to touch him, to make sure he was still there.

"What's the matter, Stub?" he asked tenderly. "Funeral today get to you?"

"Yes," she admitted. "What if that had been you, Ed? What would I do without you?"

Reaching over, he took her in his arms. "You'd cope, honey, you'd cope. You're a tough little girl, and I know you could handle it."

Marion wasn't so sure, but she kept her doubts to herself.

8

Not many months later a letter from Mother Dorothy forcefully reminded Marion that sudden death was not limited to the mission field. "While you are so far away, I hesitate to give you such sad news, but I know you will want to share my grief. Your brother, Chuck, died suddenly of a heart attack last week."

Marion could hardly believe it. Her only brother, dead at 34! She remembered his concern for her, his visits in Hartford and Rocky Hill, and his teasing laughter. She wept for all the years she had really known him so little and for the years ahead when she would no longer have the opportunity to know him better. Ed seemed to understand her grief, and several times that week he reached for her hand and just held it, letting her know that he was right there for her, strong and protective. In his touch, Marion took great comfort.

After the tragic incident, Dorothy kept in touch more regularly as if to cling to the one child she had left. Marion felt relieved when Dorothy later wrote that Virginia, a friend who lived with her, had been such a comfort since Chuck's death. At least Dorothy wasn't totally alone in her grief.

The first five-year term at Pakistan Union High School flew by. Ann started first grade, Alice continued elementary school, Mary Ellen began academy at Vincent Hill School in India, and Ed became principal.

The last year of their term, the Hutchinsons were the only foreigners on campus. Marion missed the fellowship of other Americans, but found herself drawn closer to the national staff. Visiting in their homes, she soon discovered that some needed extra help and encouragement. One family with six children had real difficulty providing for so many on a single salary. Trying to help without wounding their pride, Marion frequently arranged to purchase more fresh produce than she needed so she would have an excuse to ask them to help eat it before it spoiled.

One day the wife, Shireen, came visiting, her thin duputta-scarf pulled over her tear-stained face. "Marion," she declared, "you are an angel."

Marion pulled back in surprise. Then she laughed. "I'm lots of things, Shireen, but not an angel. My mother used to say she thought there was a little of the devil in me. But why did you say that?"

Shireen inched forward on the couch. "Isaac would be angry that I tell you this," she confessed, "but when you sent the food today, we had nothing in the house to eat. Not *anything*! And payday isn't until tomorrow. I didn't know what to do, and I prayed, 'God, send Your angel to provide food for this family.'

"Right after that, Rahmet drove up in a horse-drawn tonga. He had a bag of potatoes, a hundred oranges, and some eggplant. He said you'd told him to drop them off at our house on the way home from market. And so," she concluded simply, "I know you are an angel from the Lord. Thank you so much, Marion. God told you to send the food today."

"I asked the Lord to use me in His work," Marion wrote to her parents, "but I seldom see such plain evidence that He is answering my prayers."

Thrilled with the letter, Cora told her church friends about the incident and the members of the Hartford Adventist Church felt they really had their own missionary out in southern Asia.

Both Ed and Marion taught classes whenever necessary and soon earned the respect and love of their students. Prof, as they called Ed, delighted them with his frankness and dry wit. After one know-it-all had interrupted class with a rather lengthy argument, Prof remarked off-handedly, "You know, we *Homo sapiens* take great pride in believing we are rational beings." The resulting laughter ended the discussion.

Everyone soon learned that Prof was unpredictable. They never knew where he'd show up. Couples who tried to meet secretly fled when he emerged from the shrubs behind them. Students who leaped over the wall to get back on campus after an illegal outing jumped right into his arms. Of course, Marion thought he ought to be at home in bed, but his midnight wanderings foiled many a student's escapade.

He spent more time than usual, however, with a bright college student named Shafqat, who seemed obsessed with a desire for Katherine's company. Katherine, of course, belonged in the girls' dormitory and in the culture of the Punjab, boys and girls were strongly discouraged from even speaking to one another privately, much less meeting.

Caught in a clandestine rendezvous, Shafqat was punished by being assigned to work with the construction crew for a week.

Perhaps during the night Ed remembered his own difficulties courting Marion, because at flag raising the next day he ordered Shafqat to his office. Fearfully, the boy appeared.

"Get your books and go to class," Ed ordered, "and after class, come sweep my office. Then do this filing. Just stay where I can see you, understand?"

Shafqat understood and gratefully resumed classes, working in the principal's office that week. When Prof left the office to repair a balky car engine, he took Shafqat with him and showed him how to adjust a carburetor.

Everything soon returned to normal, and the episode was forgotten, Shafqat thought. But on the day Katherine left school at the term's end, Prof wisely assigned Shafqat the job of standing at his office door all day to pass out ballpoint pens to students who came to get leave passes. By the time the job was finished, Katherine was gone!

Ed hated the fad haircuts the young men were getting that year. Students, usually so sharp-looking and neat, sported long, unruly hair styles. Following Prof's discussion of the matter at men's dorm worship, eight of the fellows, laughing at their cleverness in outwitting the principal, showed up with shaved heads. They had done away with long hair as he'd insisted—but still had distinctive styles that caused even more disruption in classes.

Ed called them all in. "OK, fellows," he said, "I see you got rid of the long hair, but now you have it a bit too short. Since your appearance is disrupting classes, I'll just let you work until your hair grows out." And they did.

While Ed had his encounters with the students, Marion had some of her own as she struggled to teach a high school English class that had been given her after a regular teacher came to teach the overseas elementary school. One day she soundly scolded a student for failing to turn in his assignment.

He stood respectfully, and summoning his best English, he replied, "Please do not bark at me."

The class howled with laughter. The boy looked baffled. Marion tried to help. "You can't say that, Bashir."

He looked indignant. "Why not? I say 'please' very polite!"

Because Prof always seemed to know just what was going on among the maintenance and construction crews from the village, ordinarily lazy workmen got busy when he was on campus. The head "mistri" or carpenter, a very capable Muslim man, was nevertheless prone to pad his own pocket with kickbacks from the hardware merchants.

One day when he presented Ed with an exorbitant bill for an order of nails, the principal looked him right in the eye. "And how much of this went into your pocket, Khushi?"

Khushi's eyes fell, and he reached into his pocket and laid 10 rupees on the desk.

"Thank you," Ed said gravely. "Let's adjust the bill, shall we?"

Although he tolerated no nonsense, he treated everyone with respect and thus maintained theirs. One day, annoyed with something a staff member had done, Ed reprimanded him before the students. The teacher left the class, angry and disgraced. All the campus buzzed with the incident, and everyone wondered if the teacher would resign.

The next day Prof and the teacher met with the class. "I need to apologize to Mr. Shamir," the principal said. "I did not properly understand the situation and lost my temper. Even if I'd been right, I shouldn't have said anything to him in front of all of you. As it is, I'm wrong, and I want to ask his forgiveness publicly because I reprimanded him publicly. He is one of our most valuable instructors, and I'm truly sorry for what I said."

Mr. Shamir reached for Prof's hand and shook it, accepting his apology.

The incident deeply impressed the college students. Years later one of them would report that after making a mistake, he also had apologized to his students because he remembered that as important a man as Prof was, he admitted an error and apologized publicly.

With so much going on, time passed rapidly, and in 1962 Ed and Marion returned home for a combined furlough and study leave at Andrews University. During that year, Ed planned to get his master's degree in school administration. All three girls enjoyed attending a "real school" and learning about football, Barbie dolls, and hot fudge sundaes. During vacations they visited relatives and enjoyed staying with Grandma and Grandpa Holmberg for a while. Cora could hardly believe how the children had grown. Why, Andy could hardly bounce them on his knee anymore! Watching Cora and Andy with the girls, Marion thought of how much Dorothy was missing.

In her next letter to her real mother, Marion suggested that Dorothy and her friend Virginia come to Michigan for a visit. They were delighted and as soon as their work schedules would allow, traveled to Berrien Springs. Marion scrubbed the kids within an inch of their lives and spent many days cooking and freezing goodies in preparation for her mother's visit.

During that week the girls became better acquainted with their "Aunt Dorothy." Watching them at play, Dorothy marveled at family similarities. One thing still puzzled her however—Ed's brusqueness with his family. While she could sense his love and concern for them, she never heard him say anything affectionate. He didn't even call the girls by their right names half the time.

"Hey there, Moze," he'd say, "help your Ma with the table." Or "Zip, toss the pillow to Buzz over there."

"Why does he call the girls those horrid names?" Dorothy asked Marion when they were alone.

Marion laughed. "They're nicknames he gave them to indicate their speeds. Mary Ellen always takes her time, moseying around. So she's 'Moze.' Alice likes to zip through everything in a hurry. And Ann just buzzes along, letting the world go by. So we have Moze, Zip, and Buzz.

"You've probably also noticed that I'm Stub, haven't you? It's because I'm so short and 'stubby.' Ed's funny in some ways. He doesn't want anything that smacks of sentimentality. Sometimes I wish he'd tell me he loves me, but he won't. If I ask him he says, 'Sure I love you. I sleep in your bed and eat at your table don't I?' And for him that seems to prove it."

Dorothy looked thoughtful. "Well, he's certainly different

from your father," she said. "He'd tell me several times a day how much he loved me—when he was there. But he'd go off for months without a word, and he never did provide for you kids. I think I'd rather have a fellow like Ed who puts his love into action rather than words. I've watched him fixing lunch for Ann and her friends when you're not here, and it's amazing."

Marion agreed, but she still wished that Ed would tell her of his love. Degree in hand, Ed headed back to Pakistan with his family for another five-year term. Marion had thought she was busy under Principal Hamilton's administration, but her load then was nothing compared to the work Ed piled on her. Short-staffed as usual, he added one job after another to his wife's busy day.

During that term Marion was girls' dean, food matron, secretary to the principal, English teacher, pianist for choir and church, compound hostess, Dorcas leader, and teacher for Ann and Alice. Not all these jobs came at once, fortunately, but hardly a day passed when she wasn't filling five or six positions.

Ed worked just as hard, of course. In addition to being principal, maintenance man, purchasing agent, teacher, and business manager, Ed became an ordained minister. Now he could add weddings and baptisms to his list of duties. Although he continued with his regular routine, the ordination recognized his constant ministry to the school's students and staff. Under his watchful guidance many young people gave their hearts to the Lord, determined to follow in Prof's footsteps.

"Why don't you and Virginia come visit us?" Marion wrote to Mother Dorothy in 1966. "Mary Ellen will be graduating from Vincent Hill School in India, and if you fly to Delhi, we'll pick you up and bring you back to Pakistan with us after graduation."

Intrigued by the idea, the ladies agreed. The Hutchinson family delighted in showing their guests Asia's fascinating aspects including their home in Pakistan. The girls laughed uproariously when they almost had Aunt Dorothy believing that the black buffalo gave black milk! They had great fun introducing the women to chapatties, curry, and mangoes. How far away America seemed! When departure time arrived, Dorothy and Marion felt as if they really knew each other for the first time.

While Marion grew closer to her mother that term, Ed lost his. When he received word that his mother had died, Marion and the girls helped him pack, stopping to give him extra hugs and assurances of their love. Mother Hutchinson had not been really well for years, but somehow her death seemed more tragic because her son was on the other side of the world. As soon as he could arrange a flight, Ed left to attend the funeral and comfort his father.

"I know you'll be busy," Marion said, "but you'll have a shopping list for the school. Do you suppose you could get some new shoes for the girls to wear home next year? I'd love to be in style when we get back."

"Sure, Stub. Just draw around their feet, and I'll get the shoes a bit bigger to allow for some growth before furlough."

Each girl stood patiently on a sheet of white paper while Marion traced the outline of her foot. When Ed pulled out the sheets at the Manchester shoe store, all the clerks and Ed's sister helped to select just the right shoes for the missionary's kids. To everyone's joy, the shoes did fit the next year and were right in style.

For Ed's father, his visit in the States seemed too short, but there was no talk of his staying. "You go on being a missionary, son," the old man told him. "It will be right lonesome without your ma, but I want you where the Lord needs you. We'll see you next year, anyway."

Glad to be back at his job again, Ed worked as tirelessly as ever. Under his leadership, Pakistan Union School became a four-year college. Desert King Industries became well-known for its puffed wheat and peanut butter. Students began passing the government's matriculation exams with unusually high scores, and the campus blossomed with flowers and neatly trimmed hedges. With the school running well, Ed and Marion decided to take the girls back home and introduce them to American life. Accordingly, they applied for a permanent return.

1968 found them at Andrews again with Ed upgrading his history credentials and taking classes in counseling and guidance, subjects he had often wished he knew more about when dealing with problem students. Mary Ellen, who'd been away at school, rejoined the family and finished her last year of college at Andrews. Marion loved having her home again, and got her to help design and sew new outfits for herself and the girls. When Mary Ellen fell in love with Ted, the whole family was right there to celebrate her engagement.

All that year while the family was at Andrews the General Conference refused to vote Ed's permanent return. He had been willing to go somewhere else in Southern Asia, but felt that he had given Pakistan all he had to offer there.

"But we need you back at the college," the brethren protested. "We've had only an acting principal ever since you left. When you were there, the school did better financially and scholastically than it has ever done. Won't you please reconsider?"

At last Ed agreed with one reservation. He wanted to stay in the States another six months to see Mary Ellen married. After all, a father ought to be able to officiate at his daughter's wedding!

The Missions Committee agreed, and Ed and Marion were there to take part in Ted and Mary Ellen's wedding celebration. Shortly after that, Ed helped the young couple move into their new apartment in Connecticut. Then, after many goodbye hugs, the rest of the Hutchinsons set out for the mission field again, leaving Mary Ellen to start a new life with Ted.

CHAPTER

9

Back in Pakistan, Ed began planning for the college's first four-year graduation ceremony. Students from far away East Pakistan were eagerly looking forward to returning to their families. But winds of war started blowing across the Punjab.

In 1947 Pakistan had split from India when that country had gained her independence from the British. Because the many Muslim inhabitants feared oppression from Hindu rulers, they had begged the British for a portion of India as their own. They wished to call their land "Pakistan," land of the pure, and the followers of Allah and his prophet Muhammad would rule themselves according to the dictates of Islam and the holy Koran.

This presented a problem because there were two major areas of Muslim population in India—one in the west, the other in the east. It seemed impossible to form a single country whose halves were separated by a thousand miles of Indian territory, but this is what was done. Many predicted the situation could not last, and they were right.

By the time the Hutchinsons returned to West Pakistan in 1970, East Pakistan seethed with rebellion. Those inciting the unrest claimed that East Pakistan's representatives were outnumbered in the legislature and that West Pakistan's interests seemed to take priority. East Pakistan rebels agitated for a separate nation—Bangladesh. West Pakistan, of course, refused.

Many of the school's seniors from East Pakistan had not been home since arriving four years earlier. Anxiously they watched the newspapers, hoping that they could get home after graduation.

As the media reported more and more rebel raids in East Pakistan, West Pakistanis began to show hostility toward the Bengali students at the college. Bengalis who went to town took with them Punjabi friends, letting *them* talk to shopkeepers rather than reveal their own Bengali accents.

One afternoon a visibly shaken group returned from town. They had encountered a gang of ruffians, and the Bengalis barely escaped with their lives. Some had cuts and bruises. After this, East Pakistani students stayed mainly inside the campus walls.

The war accelerated slowly. By summer of 1971, open fighting seemed unavoidable. In a surprise move, Pakistan suddenly declared that all currency notes of 50 rupees or more had been replaced. Demonetized bills must be exchanged at the bank for new ones within four days or they would be worthless. This would, the government explained, cut off the rebels' money supply by rendering their funds useless.

Panic hit the country. On campus, staff members and students alike searched out every single demonetized bill. Since 50 rupees was equivalent to only $5 at the time, no one had much valid currency at all. Daily marketing was standard procedure since there was little refrigeration on campus. Even the cafeteria bought fresh vegetables daily. Suddenly there was no money for food.

Acting quickly, Ed called an emergency staff meeting. "We all know that our money is worthless now," he began. "Unless we can exchange it at the bank, it will be worthless forever. People desperate to exchange their bills are standing in bank lines all night. There's no way the bank will be able to handle all these exchanges before the deadline.

"I suggest that all persons on campus bring their demonetized bills to the business office and obtain a receipt today. When all the money is in and counted, I'll try to get it into the bank in a single deposit. We may not get our money back for several days, but at least this way we have a chance.

"Meanwhile, we will pool our resources to make it through the next few days. If some of you have extra flour, share it. I'll talk to the vegetable sellers and see if they'll extend us credit until after this crisis. If so, I'll buy larger quantities than usual so staff families can buy on credit from the cafeteria supply. If we keep our heads and work together, none of us need suffer too badly."

The staff disbanded, relieved that someone had taken charge. That night Ed and the business office staff worked late counting and recording deposits.

Early the next morning the principal bagged the demonetized currency and drove to the village. Bank lines extended a mile from the front door. Ignoring the line, Ed drove around behind the bank and parked. Quickly he retied the top of each money bag with an extra knot and stepped to a barred side window.

"Salaam aliekum!" he called in greeting through the window. "I know you people are terribly busy today. We wanted to make things as easy as possible for you, so we collected all the campus funds ourselves. I know you don't have time to count this today, but we've dealt with you for years and know we can trust you. When you get time, count it and see if it agrees with the deposit slips inside. If not, adjust it. I'll be back next week or whenever you send me word to pick up new money. OK?"

And waiting for no arguments, Ed heaved the bags through the bars and onto the office floor and left speedily.

The wisdom of his plan was evident two days later when

the banks across Pakistan closed, and thousands of citizens were left with valueless paper currency. Newspapers published photographs of weeping businessmen standing on the Ravi Bridge, ripping up large value notes and throwing them into the river. No one on campus lost a rupee—except for the unfortunate wife who later found a now worthless 50 rupee note in the bottom of her dresser drawer where she'd hidden it!

Mounting tensions caused Ed to check the campus at night even more than usual. One night he returned to bed and was laughing so heartily Marion awoke. "What's so funny at three a.m.?" she grumbled.

Ed pulled off his shoes. "That Pathan watchman," he chuckled. "I knew when I hired him to watch the machinery that he was a tough customer. Those Pathans shoot first and question later. But I really got a scare tonight.

"He didn't know I was coming, and challenged me with a loaded rifle. What's funny is that since it's so hot, the man had taken off every stitch of clothing and stood there in the beam of my flashlight stark naked except for the cartridge belt across his chest and the rifle in his hand! He put it down when he recognized me, but I'd hate to be a man he didn't know! Now I know why I haven't caught any fellows sneaking around lately!"

Wide awake now, Marion laughed with him. Ed rested better after that, assured that the campus was well guarded.

♥ ♥ ♥

That summer, Elder Lange, the Union president, approached Ed. "Ed, we really need you in East Pakistan. You've done a terrific job here, and we'd like you to do the same thing at Goalbathan Seventh-day Adventist Academy. It's a new school, way out in the country, and their buildings now are straw and thatch. We want some good concrete construction, and the Union committee feels that you're the man for the job."

Ed hesitated. Before he'd ever agreed to return to Pakistan Union School he'd heard rumors that he might be asked to go to East Pakistan. He had questioned the brethren then, pointing out that if he were really headed there he would need to purchase different household items. They assured him he wouldn't be sent there this term. Now, a year later, they were asking him to move. How true, he thought, that a missionary's most necessary qualification is adaptability!

After praying about the matter for several weeks, he finally agreed to leave his established surroundings and pioneer in Bangladesh.

Hutchinsons' farewell grew into an elaborate affair complete with garlands, songs, feasting, and many tears. Once again Marion felt she had hugs enough to last a lifetime, but leaving the college tore at her heart. This had been home. For 12 years she and Ed had given everything they had to this school. No other place on earth could ever be quite the same.

As they drove past the big wrought iron gate and waved farewell, Marion hugged their little chihuahua, Tiny, until he yelped. Her world seemed insecure again, and she needed something to hang on to. If Ed hadn't needed both hands on the wheel to swerve around buffalo carts and bicycles, she'd have asked for one of them to hold. It was one thing to come to a quiet college campus, and quite another to go to a country that they knew was headed for an all-out war.

When they arrived in Dacca, East Pakistan, in October, they had no trouble renting in the northeast suburb of Gulshan because so many foreigners were leaving town. The Goalbathan school, 30 miles north, had no housing for them yet. Only one campus building was permanent—the principal's home. Dormitories and classrooms were thatch.

From the start the going was rough. Rebel forces occupied parts of the city, and Pakistani troops held other areas.

Traffic along main roads often had to pass through checkpoints of both armies. Meeting the Pakistani soldiers, Ed would cry, "Pakistan Zindabad!" (Long live Pakistan!) At rebel checkpoints he would shout, "Jai Bangla!" (Long live Bangladesh!) Guards from both sides smiled and let him through.

Although he laughed about it, Ed really wasn't insincere. He truly wished the best for both sides and hoped they could live in peace. He could see, however, that they were fast coming to a breaking point.

Marion and Ed were glad to find their old friends Jamile and Lois Jacobs living in West Dacca. Jacobs' daughter Lucille and Hutchinsons' Ann were best friends at Far Eastern Academy in Singapore, and the families had known each other for years.

Shortly after their arrival, Jamile drove them to Goalbathan to see where Prof would be supervising construction. With rebellion in the air, both men stayed alert for signs of trouble.

"Duck!" shouted Jamile as he slid down behind the wheel. Ed ducked too while bullets whistled past the car and splintered a tree beyond. Zigzagging, Jamile accelerated and soon passed a Pakistani army truck. Another traveled ahead. All at once the men realized that they were in the middle of a strung-out army convoy that the rebels were ambushing. That night the two families held a special session of thanks to God for His protection that day.

Once on the job, Ed spent most of his time going from shop to shop in an attempt to purchase building supplies. Materials had to be transported to the isolated mission school, and few truckers wanted to risk the trip. By arguing and paying higher rates, Ed often persuaded one to go, and bit by bit cement and bricks arrived on campus. Whenever Ed drove out to Goalbathan, Marion rode along, determined to stay close to her husband in this precarious situation.

Daytimes weren't so bad, but blackouts made the nights seem interminable. An ominous silence filled the air, a silence broken only by shellfire.

One night after Hutchinsons had gone to bed, a pounding on the door awakened them. Ed slipped on his trousers and answered it, not daring to use a flashlight because of the blackout. In the dark a steel bayonet jabbed his chest.

"Who you?" a gruff voice barked. "Why you here?"

Ed knew West Pakistani Urdu but very little Bengali. Still, he tried to explain that he was a missionary, a teacher, an American. He heard several men's voices buzzing in the darkness as they discussed his answer.

"American! American!" he repeated.

At last the bayonet withdrew along with the freedom fighters. Ed breathed a sigh of relief and bolted the door. The war was becoming very personal!

The next week en route to Jacobs' house, the Hutchinsons stopped at Dhan Mandi, a mission compound housing many national staff families. Although it was a bit out of the way, Ed felt strongly that he should check on the safety of the workers there.

As they arrived at the compound, Marion glimpsed an army truck backed up to the front gate. "What's going on?" she asked in alarm.

"I don't know, but I intend to find out," Ed said, parking quickly.

Soon Marion saw him arguing with a Pakistani officer. She leaned out the window to hear what he was saying, his Urdu coming in very handy now.

"Why are you taking away our workers?" Ed demanded. "They are Bengalis, of course, but they are loyal to the government. We mission people try to stay out of this war. We aren't supporting the freedom fighters. We just wish to carry on our work."

The officer shifted uncomfortably. "I have orders to

remove them," he said finally.

"For what purpose?" Ed persisted. "You have no right to arrest innocent citizens. I lived many years near Lahore. I know Pakistani law. Where is your arrest warrant?"

Unable to produce such a document, the officer began apologizing. He ended by climbing into the truck and ordering the driver to leave.

Inside the compound the Bengalis clustered together praying. "If you hadn't come, we would all be dead," they declared. "God must have sent you to talk to that Pakistani officer in Urdu. God bless you."

Just to be safe, the men barricaded the gate as Hutchinsons drove off. Ed grinned at Marion and gave her hand a quick, reassuring squeeze. "I think the Lord sent us here, Stub. I don't doubt that our people would have been imprisoned or killed if we hadn't come along. This war is getting too close!"

Evidently the workers thought so, too, for by morning they had disappeared into faraway villages on a two-month unscheduled leave! And nobody blamed them a bit.

As Marion and Ed drove back and forth to Goalbathan every few days with their dog, Tiny, between them, they had to stop at various army checkpoints for clearance. At one bridge they were always halted by a friendly young soldier, who told Marion one day, "You like my mother." She smiled, flattered that he thought she was like his mom.

One day when they stopped, the soldier handed Marion a red rose and gestured that she should wear it in her hair. Trusting the boy's friendship, she obliged, wondering if it was some sort of sign to hidden snipers.

On the way back that afternoon they again stopped at the bridge, but this time a new sentry halted them. "Where's the young man who was here this morning?" Ed asked.

The sentry's face fell. "He die today, Sahib. Bullet kill."

Saddened, they drove on home. Such a waste of life! Such senseless killing!

Because the Hutchinsons' rented house was near the airport, heavy shelling bombarded their area of town. The Jacobs, in the quieter western part of Dacca, began contacting them daily to be sure they were safe.

The first week of December when Jamile failed to reach Ed by phone, the Jacobs drove across the city to find them. As they neared the airport, sirens sounded. The Americans jumped into a six-foot roadside ditch and huddled there, praying while bombers strafed the airport.

By the time the Jacobs finally arrived at the Hutchinsons' place, Jamile had made a decision. "You've got to come stay with us," he declared. "I'm mission president here, Ed, and I can't let you remain in such a dangerous area. No argument. Just pack up and come right away.

"Today I heard that India has entered the war on the side of East Pakistan. We're really going to see some action now!"

So Ed and Marion packed suitcases and moved to the other side of town. It was a good thing they did, too, for Jamile was right. For 13 terrible days both sides fought with fierce intensity. The missionaries stayed together but couldn't stand waiting, doing nothing.

"We're going to scout around for food, Stub," Ed told his wife. "Be back shortly."

So Marion worried about Jamile and Ed as she and Lois sorted used clothing for welfare distribution. When shells came too close, they would leave the building and huddle behind sandbags in the yard. Concussion from the shells vibrated the doorknobs right off the doors!

♥ ♥ ♥

"*Victory! Victory! Jai Bangla!*" Joyous shouts declared the news on December 16. Liberation forces had won. East Pakistan was now Bangladesh. As Pakistani troops withdrew, roads opened again. Foreigners were still not allowed to fly into Dacca, however, as the country was awaiting the arrival of its leader, Sheik Mujibur-Rahman, who would not return from exile until January of 1972. Ann and Lucille, waiting in Singapore to come home for Christmas vacation, fretted at the delay.

When the girls finally arrived in January, there was very little vacation time left. The Hutchinsons and Jacobs joined in celebrating a belated Christmas, complete with gifts and pumpkin pie. The two families, along with the local citizens, began to relax after the stresses of war. A few short days later Lucille and Ann flew back to Singapore to finish their junior year of academy, reluctant to leave but thankful to have seen their parents even for a little while.

10

As soon as the war ended, Ed approached Marion about a change in their living situation.

"Now that things have settled down, Stub, how about moving out to Goalbathan, where I can get something done? This commuting back and forth wastes too much time."

Marion nodded. "Fine with me. I don't mind living in a thatch house if you'll just pour me a concrete slab for a floor. I don't want to carpet the ground!"

"No problem. I'll even add our big shipping box and make you a two-roomed house. How's that?"

Before long Marion had a thatch bedroom/kitchen and a packing case living room.

The water supply proved to be more of a problem. Although water ran just beneath the earth's surface, sinking a pump required time and expense. Water for most of the campus came from a single hand pump. Marion's water ran through a hose poked through her kitchen window. Hot water was no problem. In that climate, all of it was hot!

Watching the girls trying to remain modest while taking baths at the public pump every day, Ed became concerned. He had teenage daughters, and he thought some other arrangement could be made to preserve the girls' modesty. Marion also noted that most girls had only one sari, so they would wrap in something else while they washed it on Fridays, wave it half dry, and put it on clean for Sabbath.

"Why don't these girls have Sabbath saris?" she asked D. P. Rema, the principal.

He sighed. "Most of them come from very poor homes," he answered. "Furthermore, more than half of our students don't know where their parents are right now. This war has scattered everyone."

When Marion told Ed, his jaw tightened. "I'm going to fix up something for those girls," he declared.

Before long the girls' dorm had real showers. The project had required a new well and water tank, but the girls could now wash in private. Furthermore, Ed went to Dacca and came back with an extra sari for every girl in the dorm. Now they'd have Sabbath attire.

Principal Rema made good use of Marion as soon as she arrived, assigning her to teach one Bible and two English classes in the high school. They were scheduled early in the morning so that she would be done before 10:00, leaving the rest of the day free for other work such as setting up a library!

Construction progressed more smoothly as Ed began putting up a one-story industrial building composed of six rooms in a row with doors from each room into the next.

An American company had been doing some construction several miles away, but the workers were evacuated during the war. The foreman had become acquainted with Ed, and since he was leaving American machinery on the site, he asked Ed to stop by now and again to check on it.

"Of course we have a full-time watchman," he explained, "but I'd still appreciate your checking on it as you go into town, if you don't mind."

"No problem," Ed said. "It's right on my way."

So once or twice a week Ed stopped by the site and looked around. When the watchman confided that small items had begun disappearing during the few hours when he slept, Ed stopped at the police station and reported the matter. An officer promised to investigate, and Ed hurried on into town.

Back at the school in his thatched house, Ed watched Marion cooking rice and squash for supper. "You know," he commented, "for a mission wife, you're not half bad."

Marion smiled. That was as close as Ed ever got to a compliment, and its rarity made it precious. As she dished up the meal, she thought again how blessed they were. The war had ended, workers had returned from their villages, and construction was well under way. Life at Goalbathan was interesting and the work rewarding because the students really wanted to learn. If only they weren't so far from town and the Jacobs, the situation would be perfect.

Around noon the next day a messenger arrived from the Union office. He had alarming news. The Jacobs had received a telegram from Singapore—Lucille was dead.

Ed and Marion jumped into their Mazda and roared off at full speed for Dacca. Surely there must be a mistake! Lucille, the sweet Christian girl whom everyone loved—Lucille could *not* be dead!

But she was. A garbled long-distance call had revealed that on a school camping trip she had fallen into a rocky crevasse and had died before she could be rescued. Ann had tried to go after Lucille, but staff members stopped her. Although they lowered a physician down to the injured girl, he was unable to save her life.

Lois and Marion cried together and then packed suitcases for the Jacobs' flight to Singapore. The bereaved parents departed at once, leaving others to close up the house and tend to details.

With hearts aching for their friends who had already been through so much during the war, Ed and Marion headed back to Goalbathan. When the Jacobs returned, they resumed work but to those around them they still seemed in shock, hardly able to admit that they had buried their daughter in Singapore.

Later, when Ed happened to mention that it was rather ironic now that the war was over that he'd received a notice from his insurance company offering to double his life insurance at a special rate, Jamile answered very solemnly, "I think you ought to do it, Ed. If anything happened to you, Marion could use that extra money."

Surprised, Ed mailed the company a premium to double his insurance.

Whether it was the shock of Lucille's death, the dangers braved during the war, or simply that for the first time there were no children at home, Ed mellowed that spring. Marion noted with pleasure that he was spending more time in prayer and Bible study. Occasionally he read a Bible passage to her and wanted to discuss it, apparently valuing her opinion.

He also seemed to be trying to show his love in subtle ways. "I'm going into town today," he said one morning. "I'll wait till you get done with classes, and you can go with me."

"But it's Friday," Marion protested. "I have to clean house and cook."

"Well, I'll fix some food while you teach. Then when you're off, we'll go. When we get back, I'll clean the rugs for you."

Marion was amazed. Ed didn't usually consider housework his responsibility. He must really want her to go with him. Maybe he'd been thinking of their upcoming 25th wedding anniversary. Whatever caused the new attitude, Marion loved it and hoped it would last.

In April the Hutchinsons moved into the first room of the partially completed industrial building. It was a relief to finally be in the same building with a bathroom!

When Ed had to take an overnight trip to Chittagong, Marion wanted to go along, but she had classes to teach. This time Ed encouraged her to stay at her post.

"You'll be OK, Stub," he assured her. "It will be only one

night. If you have any trouble, go to the Remas' house. They'll take care of you."

That night she locked herself and Tiny in the one secure room of the industrial building and went to sleep. She was awakened by a roaring wind and sand trickling onto her face through the mosquito net. She had heard of Bangladesh cyclones, but until now had never experienced one.

Marion jumped from bed, grabbed Tiny, and dashed for the bathroom, the only room with inside walls and a concrete roof. There she sat, holding the little dog on her lap and soothing herself as much as Tiny as she assured him they were all right.

Suddenly the lights went out and left them in total darkness. A grinding, shrieking noise drove Marion to her knees. Huddling on the floor, she prayed for protection. She could not possibly get to the Remas' house, and no one could reach her, either. The air outside was filled with flying sheet metal and debris.

As the wind and rain died down, morning dawned, and Marion stumbled out of her prison and into the kitchen. Looking up she saw blue sky. The metal roofing had been twisted and torn right off.

When Ed returned he toured the campus, amazed at all the damage done in a few hours. "I'm sure sorry I was gone," he told Marion. "It must have been rough all by yourself with everything flying around. Next time I'd better take you with me." And he promptly got to work repairing the damage done to his new construction.

At the end of May, Ann flew in for summer vacation, her meeting with the Jacobs causing fresh tears over Lucille. Marion and Ed now occupied three rooms of the industrial building—the first had become a living room, the second a bedroom, and the third a kitchen. When Ann arrived she slept on a cot in her parents' bedroom rather than stay alone in the big living room with its outside door.

Ann could hardly wait for Alice to arrive from Andrews University so the family could go to India for a month's hill leave. Since Lucille's death, family time together seemed more precious.

While her mother taught, Ann followed her father around, helping him wherever she could. It was fun just being with Daddy again and coming home to Mom's good cooking. With her parents' 25th anniversary coming up, Alice was bringing a special gift for them from the States. Ann had already contributed to the festivities by bringing priceless vegetarian foods and Cadbury chocolate bars from Singapore.

Although the silver anniversary actually came on Wednesday, the party was postponed a day in hope that Alice would be there. On Thursday when she still hadn't arrived, the Jacobs and two other overseas families decided to go ahead with the celebration.

The party provided a welcome relief from the recent tragedies, and everyone enjoyed it. On the way home that night, however, reality asserted itself when a strange jeep threatened to run the Hutchinsons' Mazda off the road and chased them most of the way to Goalbathan.

Ed worried about the incident. They were 30 miles from the city and a long way from a police station. All they could do was pray for protection.

Before going to sleep that night, Ed took Marion in his arms. "It was a great party, wasn't it, Stub? You know, you've been a good wife, a good mother, and a good lover for 25 years. Do you want to sign up for another 25?"

Marion could hardly believe her ears. Her undemonstrative New Englander almost sounded romantic. "Yes, I do," she replied, holding him tightly. "But why has it taken you so long to tell me this? Half the time I feel that I don't measure up to what you want. I love you, Ed, and I can't imagine being with anyone else in the whole world."

Ed bent to kiss her. "Good," he said. "I love you too. Now let's get to bed!"

Alice finally arrived on Friday. She exclaimed over the shop building and pulled Ann's cot from the bedroom into the living room beside her own. That night the family gathered in the kitchen to enjoy a home-cooked meal made special by American treats. On Sabbath the Hutchinsons attended the school church, and the girls delightedly renewed acquaintances with friends they'd known in West Pakistan.

On Sunday Elder and Mrs. Lange, lovingly known to all as "Grandma and Grandpa Lange," arrived for a visit. As Union president, Oliver Lange had come to check on the progress of the new school.

When the Langes arrived, Marion and Ed turned over their bedroom to the elderly couple and set up cots for themselves in the living room with the girls.

Monday and Tuesday passed swiftly in a round of busy activities. After supper Tuesday, the Hutchinsons took the Langes for a drive through the countryside, pointing out places of interest to their guests. The girls took turns driving, to their own delight, of course. When they returned, the families joined in worship, with Ed and Pastor Lange asking God's blessing upon themselves and the new school. Then they retired for the night.

Shortly after midnight Tiny's frantic barking awakened Ed. Hearing voices on the porch outside, he tiptoed through the Langes' bedroom to the kitchen's outside door. Opening it, he discovered a gang of angry men waving sticks and guns.

Bandits! he thought, and ducked, but not fast enough to miss being hit on the head with one of the sticks. Dodging back into the kitchen, he raced through it and into the Langes' bedroom, slamming the bedroom door and bolting it.

"Oliver!" he shouted to Elder Lange. "Wake up! A gang's after us!" Then he dashed to a window facing the school and began calling. "Help! Rema! *Help! Bandits!*"

If anyone at the school heard him, there was little that could be done. The armed ruffians were more than a match for a few students and teachers. Elder Lange pulled on some trousers and stood guard over the bolted door. The girls and their mother joined the Langes in the bedroom, where the women pushed a heavy chest in front of the door to the kitchen.

Crashing sounds came from the other end of the building as the bandits discovered some three-inch bamboo poles and began battering the outside door of the living room with them.

Shouting at the intruders and begging them to stop, Oliver and Ed ran into the living room. All at once the top two door panels shattered, leaving a gaping hole. A Sten gun appeared in the opening, its muzzle pointed at Ed.

"Oliver! Watch out!"

Ed sprang out of the line of fire as the older missionary ducked. The gun swiveled and fired, spraying bullets in an arc.

"He's shot my leg off!" Ed shouted, dragging himself back into the bedroom before collapsing on the floor.

Alice, who had followed her father and Pastor Lange into the living room, now sprang to the older man's side. "What do they want, Grandpa?" she cried.

"The key to this door," he answered. "Where is it?"

"Here!"

"Get back to the bedroom," he ordered, and dashing to the half-broken door, he unlocked it and raced for the bedroom, bolting the door behind him.

Ed, semiconscious, lay moaning on the floor. As the women examined him, they discovered that a bullet had entered his back and come out his thigh, severing a major artery. He was losing blood fast.

In a moment the thieves, battering now at the bedroom

door, broke its top panels as well.

"Let's give them money, Grandpa," Alice called and running to the file, she returned with her hands full of bills. Pastor Lange handed them through the shattered door to the bandits. This stopped the gang temporarily as they examined their loot and ransacked the living room closet and suitcases.

Then they demanded more money. Believing the money was gone, Elder Lange yanked off his watch and passed it through the door. Then Alice knelt and took off her father's watch and her own and handed them over. Grandma Lange took hers, Ann's, and Marion's and shoved them beneath a pile of clothes.

Suddenly at the opening in the door a thin, dirty chap appeared with the terrible Sten gun and pointed it at the older missionary. Oliver Lange dodged again as the bandit pulled the trigger. This time a bullet gashed Pastor Lange's forearm before plowing into the opposite wall. He grabbed a towel, wrapped it around his wrist, and returned to the door in an attempt to pacify the intruders by handing them his briefcase.

One man appeared willing to listen to reason and finally understood that their ramming had jammed the door so that it could not be opened. Elder Lange told him that if he would go to the other end of the building and come through the kitchen, he would move the large chest and let him into the bedroom.

"Help me push this chest back," he ordered, and the women helped him clear the doorway.

Suddenly Ed began speaking. "I'm dying," he muttered and lapsed into unconsciousness again.

As the leader and four bandits entered the bedroom, Ann and Alice began a show of Eastern grief, wailing loudly. "Our father is dead," they cried. "You killed him. You killed our father. What more do you want?"

This scene seemed to sober the leader. He ordered his men outside for a few minutes. In the quiet, the group gathered around Edwin and each one prayed for him, his daughters praying confidently for his life but asking God to give them strength to bear it if He did not live.

Hardly had they finished when the gang returned, the gunman still waving his weapon restlessly back and forth. He shouted to Pastor Lange, "Buso! Buso!" (Sit down! Sit down!)

"Sit down, Grandpa," the girls begged. "Quick."

He backed up to the bed and sat down.

Pointing his gun at the safe, the leader shouted, "Money! Money!"

Quickly Marion opened the safe. Since they had both building funds and hill-leave money, there was a good bit in the safe and file. With the gun trained on her, Marion handed over checks, travelers' checks, and bundles of cash. Then the robbers demanded and received the car keys.

The girls began urging that their father be taken to a hospital. At last the leader gestured to them to take him and go. Moving Ed's heavy body required a stretcher of some sort, and Elder Lange persuaded one of the thieves to hand him one of the lightweight army cots from the living room through the smashed opening in the door.

Ignoring Ed's pleas to be left alone, the family gently lifted him onto the cot. To their amazement, the bandits helped carry him to the car and maneuver him inside.

"Go, go!" the gang leader ordered.

"We can't," Alice replied stoutly. "You have the keys." And she gestured at the ignition.

After a brief conference, the men handed over the keys.

"I'll drive," Alice declared. "Mom's in no shape to do it. She'd better sit in front with me to tell me where to go. I don't know the way. Grandma, you get in front too. Daddy's taking the whole backseat, so, Ann, you and Grandpa will have to crouch on the floor." And with that she gunned the engine and sped toward Dacca.

As they flew down the road, Marion felt numb. Surely Ed wasn't dying! Yet she felt in her heart that he really was. What would she do without him? Where would she go? Who would she be if she were not Mrs. Ed Hutchinson? Who would hold her hand? She'd never been on her own. She'd always been the Litches' welfare kid, the Holmbergs' daughter, or Ed's wife. She'd never been just Marion.

Suddenly a jackal dashed across the road. "What should I do?" Alice screamed. "I'm going to hit him."

"Hit him!" two or three ordered at once.

With a heavy thud the jackal went flying into the night as Alice, shaking with fright, sped on.

The 30 miles seemed endless, and Ed's groans and mutterings became weaker—then still. Following Marion's directions, Alice pulled up at the Mirpur mission gate and honked frantically. No one came. Everyone piled out of the car and began to climb over the gate.

Marion stopped. "Ed's alone," she called, and ran back to him. He lay still and quiet. She felt his head. It was cold. *He's dead*, she thought. *He's really dead.*

Jamile and Lois—in their nightclothes—came running out.

"Jamile, Ed's dead," Marion said flatly.

"Oh no! Surely not," he protested. "Let's get him to the hospital."

Within 15 minutes Ed lay in the Dacca hospital emergency room.

"Dead on arrival," an orderly intoned.

"No, he's not!" Marion said sharply. "Bring him back. Do something."

Carefully the doctor injected adrenaline into Ed's heart and began attempts at resuscitation. Grandma Lange stood beside Ed, her hand on his throat.

"He's not dead," she insisted. "I can feel a pulse."

"It's your own pulse you're feeling," a nurse said gently. "He really is dead."

For two hours Sylvia Lange refused to leave him, insisting that he was alive. At last Lois and Marion realized that she was in shock and asked the doctor to give her a sedative. Someone also noticed the towel around Elder Lange's arm, investigated, and stitched up his bullet wound.

Then, realizing that nothing more could be done, Jamile urged that they all go home for the night. No one said much. What was there to say? A husband was dead. A father was dead. A friend had gone.

CHAPTER
11

Early the next morning everyone helped take care of formalities and prepare for the afternoon's funeral. Embassy and police reports were filed. The American embassy arranged for a casket to be sent to Goalbathan, where Marion had requested that Ed be buried in the school graveyard.

Elder Lange drove Marion and the girls back to the school to clean up and pack. Remembering another missionary whose mate was murdered, Marion determined to exit the country quickly before she found herself caught in a trial that might keep her there for years.

They found the industrial building in shambles and the school in confusion. After the foreigners had left, the bandits had ransacked the three rooms but had taken little or nothing more. Then they invaded the girls' dormitory, attacking three of the girls. Rumor had it that the intruders came from a nearby village and that one had been heard to swear he'd "get that American" for reporting to the police the thefts from the American construction site down the road.

"I'll select a burial site and get a grave dug," Elder Lange told Marion. "You and the girls get on with your packing."

So Alice and Marion packed, but Ann felt her first task was to remove every trace of her father's blood from the floor and carpet. Fiercely she scrubbed until the stains were almost all gone.

In the afternoon carloads of guests began arriving for the funeral. Among them were Union office staff, workers from nearby towns, Baptist missionaries, the American ambassador, and the construction engineer whose previous absence had necessitated Ed's checking on his property. Friends had prepared the body for burial, and when the casket arrived, the kitchen became the funeral parlor. As he passed the coffin, the engineer broke down completely, weeping for his lost friend. The handful of flowers he laid on the coffin comforted Marion in this land without florists and funeral wreaths.

At 4:00 the casket was closed and carried to the gravesite. Students sang "Near to the Heart of God," and Pastor Jacobs read Psalm 90 and offered prayer. With an occasional break in his voice, Elder Lange managed a brief sermon on the blessed hope. Alice ended the service by offering a prayer of thanksgiving to God for such a loving and understanding father.

At the end of the ceremonies, they buried Ed Hutchinson in the Goalbathan Seventh-day Adventist Academy graveyard to await the coming of the Master Builder for whom he worked. C. H. Tidwell, one of his fellow missionaries, later wrote:

He built of bricks and mortar, of minds and souls,
buildings to last a century
characters to last an eternity.

On the drive back to Dacca, Lois Jacobs looked at Marion. "You and the girls have done so well. Everyone marveled at the way you kept your composure."

Marion faced her, drawn and weary from the ordeal. "We marvel, too," she said. "It's partly because we're numb from shock, but I feel also that the Lord has been holding our hands and giving us strength."

Lois nodded. "I'm sure He has been, but if your experience is anything like mine, you'll appreciate His hand even more during the next few months. We'll be praying for you, Marion."

The following day Marion and her daughters boarded a jet for New York City, the closest airport to Mary Ellen and Ted. Notified by the General Conference, Mary Ellen met the plane and took the emotionally battered trio to her home.

Marion moved through the next few months in a daze. Ed's salary would continue for one more year, and since the insurance company had received the premium doubling Ed's coverage just before his murder, they agreed to pay the doubled amount. With these funds, Marion decided to return to college and finish her interrupted secretarial course so that she would have a marketable skill.

July found her with the girls in an apartment at Andrews University in Michigan. Ann left for Singapore that fall, determined to graduate with her class at Far Eastern Academy. Alice enrolled for the senior year of her business course and remained with her mother.

With the shock wearing off, Marion began to realize how dependent she had always been on others. In foster homes she had been told what to do. In school she'd followed Stephanie's leadership. Then Ed stepped in, loving her in his gruff New England way, and ordering her life completely.

Cora and Dorothy tried to comfort her with calls and letters, but she still felt alone and vulnerable. Food seemed tasteless; she ate little. Naturally petite, she now grew thin and gaunt.

Alice tried to tempt her appetite. "Try this pizza, Mother. It's delicious!" "Have some of these brownies I made. Aren't they good?" But brownies only reminded her of those she'd made when she was first married and brought back wistful memories of better times.

Nights became misery as she lay awake reading until she

dropped into an exhausted stupor for two or three hours before dawn. As she tried to make sense of Ed's death, she found some consolation in the fact that many of the students he left behind had dedicated themselves to the continuation of his ministry to others, and an American family, inspired by his sacrifice, had accepted an overseas call.

Finally deciding that she must get out of the apartment more, she took a secretarial job in the daytime and worked as assistant dean in the girls' dorm in the evening. This helped divert her mind but did nothing to relieve the fears that haunted her at night. With the reemergence of her childhood insecurities, she felt totally worthless. In her depression, Marion vividly remembered the times in her life when others had pointed out what she had done wrong, what needed correcting, what wasn't satisfactory. She pictured herself as inept, bungling, shy, and unattractive. The only reason anyone hired her, she was sure, was because they felt sorry about Ed's death. It was Ed's contribution they were reaffirming, not hers.

After Ann's graduation from academy, she joined her mother and Alice at Andrews and began her first year of college. Alice, now a college graduate, worked in a nearby CPA firm.

That March Marion completed the two-year secretarial course she had begun and applied for a job at the General Conference in Washington, D.C. When a job offer came, Ann moved into the dorm, and Alice rented an apartment of her own. Despite Marion's desire for their company, she felt the girls needed more freedom to live their own lives.

After moving to a Takoma Park, Maryland, apartment, Marion began work for the Southern Asia Division office in the General Conference. Elder B. H. Stickle, Jr., who had known her overseas, was delighted to have her help. She not only knew the workers in Southern Asia, but she also knew most of the mission stations by name and was acquainted with division policies.

Before long she became Elder Stickle's executive secretary, making decisions and disbursing funds in his absence. Gradually her self-confidence grew, especially when another department head asked if she'd work for him because he had heard of her ability to make sensible decisions in a crisis.

Nights remained intolerable, however. Sleeping pills, books, late-night TV, hot drinks, relaxation exercises, prayer—all seemed useless. She began taking evening classes in library science, filling the hours and postponing the inevitable return to an empty apartment.

Weekends were the worst. Marion didn't fit in with the singles, nor was she any longer comfortable with her married friends. At the large Sligo church she got lost in the crowd. She tried the Takoma Park church. No better.

In desperation, she spoke to a coworker. "Elisa, could I go to church with you?"

Elisa's face registered surprise. "Why, do you speak Spanish, Marion? I didn't know that."

Marion shook her head. "No, I don't, but I'm not comfortable in these large churches, and your Spanish group is small. For years I went to Urdu and Bengali churches where I didn't understand the sermons. May I go with you?"

"Of course. I'll pick you up next Sabbath."

When Elisa came to the apartment to get her, she noticed Marion's piano. "Do you play?" she asked eagerly. "We have a piano at our church, but no one can play it. Can you play for us?"

Unsure of her abilities, as usual, Marion demurred. But when she arrived at the church and found there really was no pianist, she agreed to play. The Spanish members took her home with them and welcomed her so warmly that from then on Sabbath was a delight. One main requirement for her happiness was filled—she was needed. But she still longed to be loved.

Well-meaning friends introduced Marion to various eligible men, but none appealed to her. Nightly she prayed that the Lord would send her someone to love. At her age, chances seemed remote. Finally she decided that she had been praying incorrectly.

"You know I want someone to share my life with, Lord, but I've found no one. Perhaps You think it best that I live alone for the remainder of my life. If so, please give me the strength to bear it—for I can hardly stand the loneliness."

She still had the girls, of course, and they were wonderful. She still had Cora and Andy, but they were aging now. Dorothy wrote occasionally and had sent a sympathy card when she heard of Ed's death, but Marion still felt basically alone. When furloughing friends from Pakistan questioned her closely, she confided that she felt lonely and incomplete without a husband. That was putting it mildly!

One morning as Marion entered the office, Mrs. Stickle met her with some news. "Oh Marion, did you hear? It's just awful. Ruth Brown was killed by an exploding water heater at the Lahore mission. Poor Kenneth! He must be devastated!"

The news hit Marion hard. She had known Ruth and Kenneth for years, a couple a bit older than she and Ed had been, but wonderful people and friends in the work. In fact, she had eaten lunch with the Browns earlier that year when they had been home on furlough. Thinking of how she had felt at Ed's death, she sent a card to Kenneth, adding a few words of sincere sympathy.

Although she heard nothing from him personally, the office continued to receive business letters and orders from Elder Brown. Whenever they arrived, Elder Stickle passed them on to her for handling. Growing accustomed to dealing with her, Kenneth began sending his requests headed "Dear

Sister Hutchinson," then "Dear Sister Marion," and finally just "Dear Marion."

In late spring he surprised her with a personal letter. "My Dear Marion," he wrote. "Thank you for your very sympathetic card at the time of Ruth's death. Even now I find it hard to discuss. I suppose you know how that goes.

"I've been finding it very hard living alone. Life just isn't complete without a companion to share it with. Our mutual friends, the Hamels, suggested to me that you are also finding life lonely these days, and I began to wonder if there was a remedy to this situation.

"I know that I'm nine years older than you, and perhaps you will see that as an obstacle. I've always liked and respected you, and with our mutual backgrounds in Southern Asia and love of the Lord and His work, perhaps we would make a suitable team.

"I must confess that you have been much in my thoughts these past few months. I'll look forward anxiously to hearing how you feel about this matter."

For the first time since Ed's death, Marion began to feel alive again. She answered Kenneth promptly. "I have also known and respected you for many years as we worked together, and I have no objections to getting better acquainted and exploring your suggestion. I, too, have been desperately lonely. As for the difference in our ages, I feel it only makes you more attractive. I've always admired older men."

Plans had already been made for Ann, Alice, and Marion to revisit Pakistan and Bangladesh that summer. It seemed possible that she and Kenneth might get together and discuss matters during that trip.

When her friend Eloise Hamel wrote from Karachi and suggested that she bring a wedding dress just in case, Marion's heart pounded like a teenager's. Within a month of changing her prayers from demands to submission, here was a man who wanted her, who had been a wonderful husband to his first wife, who was noted for patience and kindness. Furthermore, he could completely understand both her feelings over Ed's violent death and her love of Asia, for he'd been working there 25 years.

In addition to all these things, the man needed her. He said so, and others who knew him had told her so. Since Ruth's death, friends reported, Kenneth had been unbearably lonely, playing his violin for hours every evening. His daughter Judy had come from the States to live with him temporarily, but that wasn't a permanent solution. Marriage would be permanent.

When Marion and the girls arrived in Karachi, Kenneth and the Hamels met them at the airport in the middle of the night. The others went to bed while Kenneth and Marion talked until dawn.

When the household awoke, they announced their engagement. Eloise Hamel was horrified. "You can't do that," she protested. "You need time to date, to get acquainted, to be really sure you know each other."

"We've known each other for years, Eloise," Marion reminded her, "and we want to get married."

At the gala breakfast that followed, Ann and Alice seemed dazed at the suddenness of the decision. Since Alice had been married earlier that year, and Ann had plans for a December wedding of her own, however, both girls understood about love. It appeared that the mother and two daughters would all get married in the same year.

Even after the long flight and all-night talk, Marion felt wonderful on Friday. Eagerly she made plans with Kenneth and her daughters. She had promised the girls a trip to Afghanistan and Bangladesh. Kenneth needed to stay in Karachi to finish a Week of Prayer. Why couldn't Marion and the girls meet his daughter Judy and take her with them to Afghanistan, getting better acquainted along the way?

On Sunday the girls left for Afghanistan. On Wednesday night Kenneth flew back to Lahore. Thursday morning Marion and the girls joined him, and a Thursday afternoon wedding was scheduled in the Lahore Adventist Church.

While Kenneth and Marion calmly made plans, those around them were anything but calm. Before leaving Lahore to meet Marion, Kenneth had told one of the mission wives, "I'm going to ask her to marry me. If she says yes, I'll cable you the date. Please work with Mr. Ghosh to arrange a wedding reception for us."

"For how many?" Fern Babcock asked.

"I don't know," Kenneth confessed. "You guess!"

"What do you want to eat?" she persisted.

"Oh, I don't know. Cake and things. You figure it out." And with that he left for Karachi.

Two days before the wedding, the cable announcing it reached Pakistan Adventist Seminary and College. Three of the overseas wives began planning food for the reception. It wasn't as if one could simply order a wedding cake. Here everything must be made from scratch.

Sarah Munger looked thoughtful. "I know," she announced at last. "I saw the cutest thing one time. The wedding cake layers were separated by stemmed glasses turned upside down. Under each glass was a fresh rose. Let's do that!"

The other two women agreed. June Hooper donated her only can of American-made Crisco so the icing could be really white instead of buffalo-butter yellow, and the ladies got to work.

On the day of the wedding, Sylvia Ellis found herself running behind schedule. When Fern came to pick her up, she hadn't eaten lunch. "I'll just take my plate with me and eat on the way," she decided. "Put the cake and all this stuff in the car."

Within minutes Fern was driving down the Lahore road,

and Sylvia was eating her lunch as they sped along. An hour and 20 minutes later they arrived in town, 45 minutes before the wedding. They had just enough time to set up the reception table and mix the punch.

"Where's the icing? I can't find it!" Sarah asked as she rummaged through the boxes.

Sylvia groaned. "In my refrigerator back at home! I grabbed my dinner plate and forgot that I'd planned to hold the icing. What *will* we do?"

Fern dashed to a grocery store for buffalo butter and powdered sugar. Within 15 minutes she was back at the church. Sarah began softening the butter in the punch bowl, and Fern and Sylvia tried to crush the sugar lumps with their fingers.

While Sylvia poured in the sugar, Sarah whipped the butter as they alternated between despair and laughter. Fern raced back and forth between the church and reception hall.

"They're here, they're here," she reported. "Eloise is trying to put together a bouquet for Marion out of some flowers given to her by the gardener at the public park. They're a sight! She's laughing her head off. But hurry up."

As the women worked, Fern ran back to church to urge the wedding party to slow down. None of the three women heard the ceremony for all the behind-the-scenes activity.

"They're done! They're coming!" Fern warned. "Are we ready?"

"Just in time," Sarah declared. "Both layers are iced. Now set those glasses upside down over the roses, and I'll put on the top layer."

Sylvia hastened to obey. Sarah carefully lowered the top onto the wide bases of the stemmed goblets and let out a shriek! "Oh no! The glasses are sinking right through the cake! I remember now—when we did this before, there was a round layer of cardboard under the icing on top of the second layer of cake!"

Those sinking glasses were the final straw. Sylvia and Fern collapsed on nearby chairs, laughing hysterically. Sarah removed the top layer and joined them. The wedding party, rounding the corner into the church courtyard, stopped to stare.

Wiping her eyes, Fern leaped up to intercept Marion. "The cake's a disaster," she whispered. "The glasses that are supposed to hold the two layers apart sank into it. We're going to bring it to the reception table in two pieces, set the top piece on just long enough for a picture with you and Kenneth behind it, and then snatch it off before the glasses go right through the cake. Oh, this is too funny!"

And she dashed off, leaving the bride laughing too.

"What's so funny?" Kenneth inquired in his dignified manner.

"This whole wedding," Marion giggled. "They're having trouble with the cake now. Come on, Kenneth. We need to get our picture taken with it before it sinks."

So looking a bit puzzled, Kenneth posed for the picture, wondering why Sarah snatched away the top layer so fast.

Marion circulated among the guests, looking better than she had in three years. She was vibrant and alive again. Kenneth, whose sad face had touched all the wives on the mission compound, looked 10 years younger.

In honeymoon tradition, the newlyweds spent the night at the best hotel in town. And in missionary tradition, Marion spent the next afternoon in her new home at Adventpura, canning tomatoes while they were in season!

CHAPTER

12

Perhaps in contrast to the preceding bleak years, the next few weeks were the happiest Marion could ever remember. Never had she felt so loved and cherished. A dozen times a day Kenneth told her of his love, and he was continually reaching for her hand. "You don't know how happy you make me, Marion," he told her. "I was so lonely before you came. I feel like a different person now."

Both newlyweds looked different—younger, more carefree, more relaxed, and definitely happier. Fellow missionaries smiled when they heard that Kenneth and Marion had taken off on a motorcycle for a 200-mile trip to the mountains!

"Why did you marry me, Kenneth?" Marion asked. "I'm not all that pretty, you know."

Kenneth looked astonished. "I think you're beautiful now," he answered, "but when Ruth and I had lunch with you in Washington, you weren't pretty. You looked lost and pathetic. Then when Ruth died, I felt exactly that way myself. And I thought, *Somebody ought to make that girl smile again*. So I decided to do it—and make myself happy in the process."

With renewed vigor the couple threw themselves into the mission work. Kenneth edited a magazine, and Marion taught the overseas school or did secretarial work. Judy, Ann, and Alice had all returned to the States, glad that their parents were so happy together.

When the Terry Butler family left on furlough, they asked Marion to keep an eye on their empty house. She agreed, and a week after their departure, sent her gardener, Nazir, over to air the place a bit. He returned with a puzzled face. "Memsahib, something has been in that house. I found water on the floor and messes, too. The Butlers' bed is messed up. I cleaned up, but something's wrong."

In a hurry to get to the office, Marion hardly listened. "Glad you cleaned it up. Next time you go over, see if there's any more mess."

A few days later Nazir checked again. "Memsahib, Butlers' house be all messy again. Bed messed up. Floor messed up. I look all around, no see anything. I not like go there again."

Marion laughed. "You afraid, Nazir? Come on. Let's go look together."

In the Butlers' house, Marion walked into the bedroom. The bedspread that Nazir had just straightened was pulled down and scrunched up again. Cautiously she began looking under and behind the furniture while Nazir did the same in the living room.

Suddenly she noticed a curtain moving. "Nazir! Come quick! Something's on the window sill behind the curtain."

With a stout stick in his hand, Nazir tiptoed in. Carefully he pulled back the drape. Marion shrieked. An enormous three-foot lizard sat glaring at them from the window ledge.

"Don't kill him," she ordered. "Let's just get him outside."

Working together, they shooed the monster out the side door and into the drainage ditch.

Nazir grinned. "Now you believe, huh, Memsahib?"

Marion nodded apologetically. "Yes, Nazir. Now I believe!"

Telling Kenneth later, Marion suddenly realized that for the first time she had dealt calmly and rationally with a reptile.

Not bad, Marion, she told herself, *not bad at all.*

The routine of their lives was broken when Marion flew to Karachi Hospital for emergency gall bladder surgery. Hardly was she on her feet again when a call arrived from Mary Ellen. "Mother," she said in the far-off voice of overseas calls, "Grandma Holmberg just called. Grandpa has had a massive stroke, and she needs help taking care of him."

"I'll be there as soon as I can," Marion replied. "Tell Mother I'm coming."

With his forehead puckered in a worried frown, Kenneth took his wife to the airport. "You will hurry back, won't you, dear?" he asked anxiously. "I don't know how I'll manage while you're gone. I need you, too, you know. But I know your father needs you most right now. I'll share—but hurry back to me."

Suddenly Marion felt almost too needed!

When Marion landed in New York, Mary Ellen broke the sad news that Andy had passed away. Marion hurried to Connecticut to comfort Cora and plan the funeral. As she sat in the funeral parlor and listened to sympathetic murmurings, Marion remembered the big, quiet man drilling her on multiplication tables, bringing home daily surprises, rescuing a teenage runaway, and holding her hand protectively in his as they walked together.

"Thank You, God," she prayed. "Thank You for giving me such a loving, caring father."

Living at home during the month after the funeral, Marion noticed that Cora had reverted to treating her like a child, telling her when to eat, when to get up, and when to go to bed.

"I resent being ordered around," she told Mary Ellen. "I must be getting too independent. It's time I get back to

Kenneth before I get any worse!"

Two months after she left Karachi, Marion was back in Kenneth's arms, telling him everything. Since their marriage she had begun telling him all about herself, revealing her innermost feelings about her adoption and early life, feelings she never before had put into words.

With great interest Kenneth had listened to his wife, making insightful comments as she went along. Now while she was gone, he had written part of her life's story, surprising her with it when she returned. Reading it, she began to realize more than ever how much her early life had affected her attitudes and actions, and she loved Kenneth for taking the time to put her life in perspective.

It was still hard for her to accept compliments, however. When Kenneth told her of his love or how good her cooking was, she would invariably protest, "Oh, you're just saying that!" or "I'm not *that* good a cook." It took a long time for her to realize that Kenneth really did love *her*—not her actions or her cooking or her piano playing but herself. Even then she had to struggle to bring herself to thank him for a compliment or mentally assent to her own worth when it was pointed out.

At the end of their term in Pakistan, Kenneth and Marion decided to stay in the States. Mother Cora, Mother Dorothy, and Marion's dear old Aunt Doris needed family closer than Pakistan. So the Browns moved to Kenneth's old home in Nebraska and pastored four churches.

When Cora became too ill to remain at home, Marion brought her to Nebraska, where she died. After flying back to Connecticut to bury Cora beside Andy, Marion traveled to Florida to visit her real mother. Perhaps because she no longer had to balance her affections between two mothers, Marion—for the first time—felt free to give her love fully to Dorothy.

During their week together, mother and daughter talked

and talked, trying to make up for lost years. Out of these discussions came a new love and respect. When Virginia called six months later to inform her tearfully that Dorothy had died in her sleep, Marion's first thought was of thankfulness for their happy days together in Florida.

With no more elderly relatives to care for, the Browns volunteered for a two-year assignment in Korea, where they ran the servicemen's center and taught English. Marion enjoyed cooking for 20 to 40 soldiers every weekend. They made her feel *very* needed. Kenneth kept busy planning meetings, giving Bible studies, and teaching English.

When they returned to the States and attempted to retire, neither one was really satisfied. Leaving the lovely retirement home they had built in Washington, they returned to the Kansas-Nebraska Conference and began pastoring again. Grateful members welcomed them back, enjoying their home visitation and the many stories the Browns tell of God's leading in their lives.

"I know I'll never be free of my past," Marion admits, "but with the Lord's help, I'm managing the present. And I know from experience that whatever crisis yet lies ahead, the Lord will be right there with me, still holding my hand as He has all my life."

Stories of God's Healing Grace

The Heart Remembers
A daughter, mother, and grandmother find themselves separated by a painful past. Withholding forgiveness from each other as punishment, they realize that their cherished grudges have locked them away from the very people they need most. Written by Helen Godfrey Pyke, this poignant story demonstrates how God's unconditional love can free us to forgive. Paper, 108 pages. US$7.95, Cdn$9.95.

A Rose for Bethany
Beth had believed Cole loved her. But now doubt crowded her mind. Was he inconsiderate of her feelings, just like her dad? Or could it be—in spite of her resolutions—that she was acting like her father, misunderstanding the one who loved her most and throwing something special away? A love story by VeraLee Wiggins with special emphasis on recovering from codependency. Paper, 157 pages. US$7.95, Cdn$9.95.

The Heart and Soul of Landon Harris
It had all been a mistake, Landon thought. Leaving Joetta, marrying power-hungry Diana, then divorcing her. Spending 15 years in that cutthroat engineering job. All that mattered now were his son and stepson, and that he might lose them. A compelling story about a single father's quest for God and new beginnings with his family, written by Helen Godfrey Pyke. Paper, 140 pages. US$7.95, Cdn$9.95.

Stories of Triumph Over Tragedy

Forsake Me Not

First Megan lost her mother, then Alan. Would this accident take Mike from her, too? Having learned that God will never leave her, she pleads with Him for help. His answer, though not what she expects, is beyond her wildest dreams. By Kay Rizzo. Paper, 156 pages. US$7.95, Cdn$9.95.

When the Lilacs Bloom

When Mac left for Vietnam he promised Meg he'd be back when the lilacs bloomed. He wasn't. Could she ever love again? How would she raise two small children without him? How could she let go of the past? Shattered by grief, Meg clings to God's promise, "My grace is sufficient for you." Her experience is a powerful testimony to God's healing love and strong assurance that He will see each of us through every trial in life. By Sharon M. Davis Messer. Paper, 123 pages. Call your Adventist Book Center for price.

Because of Patty

They told her to put the infant girl in an institution. But a mother's love, hope, and faith continued against all odds. Read how a handicapped child became a joy to her family and a blessing to the community. Written by Patty's sister, Paula Montgomery. Paper, 126 pages. US$7.95, Cdn$9.95.

To order, call **1-800-765-6955** or write to ABC Mailing Service, P.O. Box 1119, Hagerstown, MD 21741. Send check or money order. Enclose applicable sales tax and 15 percent (minimum US$2.50) for postage and handling. Prices and availability subject to change without notice. Add GST in Canada.